WADSWORTH PHILOSOPHERS SERIES

ON

HEIDEGGER

Patricia Altenbernd Johnson
University of Dayton

Australia • Canada • Denmark • Japan • Mexico • New Zealand • Philippines
Puerto Rico • Singapore • Spain • United Kingdom • United States

Printed in the United States of America
1 2 3 4 5 6 7 03 02 01 00 99

For permission to use material from this text, contact us:
Web: www.thomsonrights.com
Fax: 1-800-730-2215
Phone: 1-800-730-2214

For more information, contact:
Wadsworth/Thomson Learning
10 Davis Drive
Belmont, CA 94002-3098
USA
www.wadsworth.com

ISBN: 0-534-57597-8

Contents

1
Pathways

Martin Heidegger's thought is controversial. Some judge him to be one of the greatest, if not the greatest, twentieth-century philosopher. Others find his thinking mystifying and even exacerbating. Some judge his language to be exciting and stimulating, and others think it totally meaningless. Some believe his political connections with the Nazis totally discredit his philosophical thought; others see no connection between the two. In September of 1966, Heidegger gave an interview to the German magazine, *Der Spiegel*. At the end of the interview, he said,

> *But the greatest need of thought consists in this, that today, as far as I can see, there is still no thinker speaking who is 'great' enough to bring thought immediately and in clearly defined form, before the heart of the matter, and thereby set it on its way. For us today, the greatness of what is to be thought is too great. Perhaps the best we can do is to strive to break a passage through it – along narrow paths that do not stretch too far.* (Sheehan 65)

Heidegger judged his own contributions to philosophy to be significant. Students in his classes report that he would sometimes come to class with a single sentence that he had written and express his judgment of the beauty and importance of the sentence. Yet, in this interview ten years before his death, Heidegger's self-evaluation seems more modest. Heidegger understands his task as following a pathway in the hope that it will provide direction for him and others.

Heidegger's life can be described as a winding pathway, full of turns and forks. At each fork in the way, he made choices. Decisions cannot be taken back, but new turns can be made on the path that lies ahead. The questions for contemporary thinkers are: Is the way that Heidegger opened worth following? If so, how should we travel along this way?

Beginnings in Messkirch

Martin Heidegger was born on September 26, 1889, in Messkirch, Baden-Württemburg. His father, Friedrich Heidegger (1851-1924), was a master cooper and the sexton of the Catholic parish. His mother, Johanna Kempf (1858-1927), was from a farm family in Göggingen. Her family had been on the same land for centuries. Martin was their first child. The family later included two other children, Marie and Fritz. They were comfortable, neither rich nor poor. Heidegger spent a great deal of time during his early childhood on his mother's family farm and may have developed his love for country paths at an early age. The family was Catholic, and Heidegger's educational path was greatly influenced by this identity.

Heidegger attended elementary school in Messkirch. He was an excellent student and was selected as a candidate for the priesthood. At that time in Germany, a Catholic boy from the country who was headed for a career in the Church, could only receive the necessary classical education by leaving home and attending a classical grammar school. In order to gain entrance to such a school, the student needed to learn Latin, which was not taught in the local country schools. Camillo Brandhuber, the local priest, taught Heidegger Latin and so helped him to gain entrance to the Jesuit grammar school in Konstanz. Heidegger spent three years in Konstanz and three more years at the Jesuit Bertholds Gymnasium in Freiburg.

In "A Recollection" written in 1957, Heidegger says of those six years, " I acquired everything that was to be of lasting value" (Sheehan 21). He reports that he studied Greek, Latin, and German languages. In 1907, Conrad Gröber, the headmaster of the school and later the archbishop of Freiburg, gave Heidegger a copy of Franz Brentano's *On the Several Senses of Being in Aristotle*. This gift motivated him to read Aristotle and set the direction for his philosophical thought. He explains this gift as the beginning of a quest.

> *The quest for the unity in the multiplicity of Being, then only obscurely, unsteadily, and helplessly stirring within me, remained, through many upsets, wanderings, and perplexities, the ceaseless impetus for the treatise Being and Time which appeared two decades later.* (Sheehan 21)

Heidegger also began to read Hölderlin during these years of his education. These early influences on the development of his thinking remained with him throughout his life.

From Theology to Phenomenology

Heidegger completed his studies at Freiburg with the intention of joining the Jesuits and moved to their novitiate in Feldkirch, Austria. He remained in the novitiate for about two weeks and was dismissed for reasons of health. He had a weak physical constitution and so was judged not fit for the physical demands of life in the religious order. He returned to Freiburg in 1909 and entered both the Jesuit seminary and the University of Freiburg. From 1909 until 1911, he studied theology and also read extensively in philosophy. In 1911, the health problem, diagnosed as nervous heart problems, reoccurred. Heidegger was advised to discontinue his studies and rest. During this period of rest, he decided not to become a priest and left the seminary.

Heidegger returned to Freiburg in the winter of 1911, intending to study mathematics and natural science. While he continued to attend lectures in these areas, he did not take the examinations. Instead, he took his examinations in philosophy and wrote his doctoral dissertation under the direction of Arthur Schneider on *The Doctrine of Judgment in Psychologism*. He completed this work in 1913.

With the event of World War I, Heidegger's life began to include a series of political choices that would also be fundamental to his life's path. In 1914, he enlisted in the military. His health again prevented him from carrying out this choice. He was dismissed. In 1915, he was called up to work in Freiburg with the Control Board of the Post Office, censoring mail. He may have read correspondence of his colleagues during this period (Ott 83). In 1918, at the very end of the war, he was drafted and served in the meteorological service on the Western Front

During this period, Heidegger began to read Edmund's Husserl's work in phenomenology. This was a new approach to philosophical thought. Heidegger believed that Husserl's method, especially if directed toward Aristotle's philosophy could prove helpful in the development of the questions that Brentano's work had already raised. Heidegger wanted to go to Göttingen to study with Husserl, but the war and his economic situation prevented this move. However, he was able to continue work at Freiburg during this period and completed his habilitation. In the German system of higher education, habilitation is further graduate work that demonstrates a thinker's abilities to conduct research and to present lectures. This is a necessary step for obtaining a faculty appointment at a university.

Heidegger hoped to receive appointment to a Chair in Christian Philosophy at Freiburg. At least in part because of this hope, he turned his research to the medieval philosopher Duns Scotus. Heidegger wrote his habilitation dissertation, *Duns Scotus' Doctrine of Categories and Meaning.* He presented his qualifying lecture on "The Concept of Time in History." In his résumé from this period Heidegger proposes the direction for his life's work,

> *This work...gave me the idea for a comprehensive account of medieval logic and psychology in the light of modern phenomenology, which would also take into account the historical significance of individual medieval thinkers. If I am fortunate enough to be admitted to the service of scholarship and teaching, I shall devote my life's work to the realization of these projects.* (Ott 86)

Heidegger set out in this direction and began to lecture at Freiburg while working as a censor at the Post Office. His first course was offered in the winter of 1915/1916 on the topic, "Principles of Ancient and Scholastic Philosophy," lectures that focused on the philosophy of Parmenides. He also lectured on Kant, Fichte, and nineteenth-century philosophy and taught a seminar on Aristotle. However, when the decision was made, the position in Christian philosophy was not given to Heidegger nor was he offered any other paid position at Freiburg.

In 1916, Edmund Husserl was appointed to a senior position in philosophy at Freiburg and so Heidegger was provided with the opportunity to work with Husserl. Opinions differ as to how long it took Husserl and Heidegger to develop a working relationship. Heidegger thanks Husserl in a personal letter for helping him publish his dissertation on Duns Scotus. However, Husserl writes a rather reserved letter of recommendation to Paul Natorp in late 1917 regarding Heidegger's suitability for a position at Marburg, and

Heidegger does not receive the position. Sometime late in 1917 Husserl and Heidegger began to discuss philosophy together and developed a cordial relationship. By the time Heidegger received orders in July of 1918 to report for duty as a meteorological observer, Husserl was writing letters to Heidegger that were friendly and even paternal in tone.

On March 21, 1917, Heidegger married Thea Elfride Petri. She was a student of economics at the University of Freiburg and a Lutheran. The marriage took place in the university chapel of the Cathedral of Our Lady in Freiburg under wartime dispensations relating to weddings. While Petri had apparently discussed the possibility of conversion, she did not join the Catholic Church. It was assumed that children from the marriage (there were two, Jörg born in 1919 and Hermann born in 1920) would be raised Catholic.

Other events of life-long significance happened during this same period. In 1917, Heidegger lectured on the protestant theologian Schleiermacher's *Addresses on Religion*. Schleiermacher's work on hermeneutics greatly influenced Heidegger. He also began an important relationship and correspondence with Karl Jaspers. It is not clear how all of these events worked together on Heidegger's thought. What is clear is that Heidegger had distanced himself from his Catholic identity by January of 1919. That same year Husserl convinced the University of Freiburg to provide a paid position for Heidegger as Husserl's assistant, and Heidegger began lecturing and assisting Husserl. Heidegger's reputation as an exciting young teacher began to develop and spread and he began the work that would culminate in *Being and Time*.

Husserl took great interest in Heidegger's development. One story tells of Husserl spending his own money to purchase the works of Luther for Heidegger. However, as he practiced phenomenology as Husserl's assistant, Heidegger took a direction that set him on a different course from Husserl. He believed that the real insight in phenomenology was to recognize an attitude of thought that had been concealed by modern scientific and technological thought. He hoped that using the method of phenomenology in reading the Greeks, especially Aristotle would help contemporary thinkers revitalize thought and overcome the spiritual crisis of the twentieth century. In 1922, a position at Marburg again became available. Husserl's recommendation commended Heidegger, and this time Heidegger received the appointment.

5

The Marburg Years

Heidegger's years at Marburg (1923 to 1928) were an extremely creative period. He lectured to excited audiences. Hans-Georg Gadamer reports that Heidegger began his lectures at seven in the morning and still had full classes. In addition to teaching, he entered into discussions with his colleagues. Especially influential were his weekly conversations with the Protestant theologian, Rudolf Bultmann. These conversations influenced Heidegger's thinking and also helped shape Bultmann's theological work and influenced much Christian theology.

During the period in Marburg, Heidegger also entered into a philosophical and personal relationship with Hannah Arendt. Arendt was Heidegger's student at Marburg. He was thirty-five and she eighteen. She became his lover as well as his student. Arendt was Jewish, and their personal relationship was broken during World War II. Arendt developed phenomenology in a political direction that is influenced by Heidegger's thought and helped to popularize Heidegger's work in the United States. Despite Heidegger's connections with the Nazis, Arendt renewed the friendship after 1950. Their relationship has received attention in recent years, and there are a number of good sources available for further reading.

While at Marburg, Heidegger wrote *Being and Time*. This philosophical work is certainly one of the most important of the twentieth century, yet it was written and published with a great deal of haste. Heidegger's lectures at Freiburg served as the beginning for the work. In 1926, when there was a possibility that he could be appointed to a chair in philosophy at Marburg that was being vacated by Nicolai Hartmann, Heidegger focused his effort on getting the manuscript written. He spent three months in the spring of that year working intensely in a cabin near his home in Todnauberg. At one point, Husserl joined him and they discussed some of the sections of the book. While Husserl would later see the work as a betrayal of phenomenology, in 1926 he still thought that Heidegger was his most important pupil and helped Heidegger with page proofs. Heidegger's book was published in 1927 in an incomplete form, and it was never completed. Chapters 2 and 3 provide an introduction to *Being and Time*.

In 1928 Husserl retired, and Heidegger was selected as his successor. Heidegger returned to Freiburg and to lecture halls filled with hundreds of students.

6

Freiburg and National Socialism

While Husserl was instrumental in helping Heidegger gain the position at Freiburg, it immediately became clear that Heidegger did not view himself as simply continuing Husserl's work. In 1929, Heidegger delivered his inaugural lecture, "What is Metaphysics?" which precipitated a break with Husserl. In the same year, he entered into public discussions with Ernst Cassirer and published *Kant and the Problem of Metaphysics*. He also published *The Essence of Reasons* and lectured on the pre-Socratic philosophers, the German idealists, and Plato's *Republic*. In 1930 he was offered a position in Berlin but turned it down because of his love for the country and his dislike of large cities.

While the move to Freiburg seemed to be the step that would put Heidegger on the path to philosophical greatness, it proved to be the step that most tested and changed his life. The political events of this period are well known. In January of 1933, Hitler was appointed Chancellor of Germany and quickly suspended the constitution and individual rights. In March, he became dictator and began to institute anti-Semitic policies. In April of 1933, Heidegger was elected Rector at Freiburg and shortly after officially joined the Nazi party. He held the position for a year, resigning in April 1934. He did not resign his membership in the party.

This event has deeply influenced the reception of Heidegger's thought. His political activities raise serious questions about his philosophical thought. Certainly Heidegger had always been politically conservative and opposed communism. Some find in Heidegger's earliest work the seeds of Nazism. Others sympathize with the situation in which he found himself and judge his actions to have been misguided, but naïve. They do not think his philosophical work should be read in the light of this political choice. They see no clear connection between the philosophy and politics. Many books have been written on this topic. While it is not possible to resolve this issue in a brief introduction, a bit more information is helpful. Several of the works listed in the Bibliography will also provide a starting point for further exploration of the relation of Heidegger to National Socialism.

It is quite clear from accounts from some of Heidegger's closest associates that Heidegger was politically drawn to National Socialism. He believed that it would be able to address the spiritual crisis of the times. Heidegger was not alone in believing that there was such a crisis. Indeed, many of Heidegger's students were compelled by his

7

thought because they found in his work a way of addressing the crisis. Karl Moehling, in "Heidegger and the Nazis," suggests that Heidegger's error may have been "his belief that an authoritarian government would be able to re-establish the unity of spirit and state which had been split apart by the arrival of modernity" (Sheehan 41). Heidegger seemed to think that in becoming Rector he would be in a position to reform German universities in a way that would align them with the spiritual needs of the German people.

By Heidegger's own account, he had determined by early 1934 that his intellectual positions were having no influence on National Socialism and that he must resign from the position as Rector. He did resign when the Nazis demanded that he fire the deans of the schools of medicine and law. He also refused to participate in the installation of his replacement. He returned to lecturing. In 1935 he delivered "The Origin of the Work of Art" and in the period between 1934 and 1942 he lectured on Hölderlin and Nietzsche. These lectures and well as his lectures on language can be understood as resistance activities as Heidegger suggests. But careful reading of Heidegger can also produce a reading that suggests his work was supportive of Nazi ideas. Even after 1934, there are reports that he continued to wear the swastika and give the salute at least as late as 1936. Karl Löwith and Hans-Georg Gadamer, early students and associates make these claims. However, Walter Beimel, who would have attended lectures in the early 1940s reports that Heidegger did not use the German salute. No one interpretation of these events seems fully satisfactory.

In 1944, Heidegger was designated as quite dispensable at the university and was drafted into the *Volssturm*, army reserves composed of old men and young boys. He was assigned to dig anti-tank ditches along the Rhine. Perhaps ironically, at the end of the war during the French occupation in 1945, Heidegger was again ruled dispensable. This time Heidegger's political judgment was more realistic. He knew that his association with the university was at risk. He applied for emeritus status. This would mean that he would no longer teach, but he would retain research status. The university de-Nazification committee determined that Heidegger could be judged to be a Nazi only during the period in which he served as Rector and recommended that his request be granted. The French authorities refused the request. He was denied teaching privileges but not dismissed, perhaps because of the influence of Jaspers. He continued in the employ of the university as a research professor. In 1950, his right to teach was reinstated, and in 1951 he received emeritus status.

With the exception of the letters that he wrote in relation to the de-

Nazification process and an interview that Heidegger gave to *Der Spiegel* in 1966, he remained silent about his relationship to Nazism. The interview was not published until after his death, so no further questions were possible. In 1983, Heidegger's son published "Facts and Thoughts." This is Heidegger's reflection on the rectorate. It was left to his son to be published at an appropriate time and is taken by some as a form of apology. It might be easier to judge the extent to which Heidegger's thinking is really compatible with authoritarian political structures if Heidegger had said more. Hans-Georg Gadamer says of Heidegger,

> *Here was a man whose thinking held a half-century in its spell, a man who radiated an incomparable power of suggestion, who as a thinker discovered the "care-structure" of existence in all the behavior of humans toward one another and the world, and (inextricably bound to it) man's tendency toward self-destruction. Yet this man could also, in his own behavior, lose himself in delusions.* (Rockmore 368)

His silence is shameful, but his silence is not a reason for refusing to read Heidegger. Nor is it reason to think that there is nothing worthwhile in Heidegger's thinking. It is a reason for keeping open the question about the political implications of his thought and the direction that it sends our own thoughts. It is a reason for recognizing that philosophy and politics cannot be viewed as totally distinct. The philosopher lives in a world that is political and has responsibility within that world.

After the War

After the hearings in 1945 and a brief period that was probably a nervous breakdown, Heidegger returned to his philosophical work. He wrote "The Letter on Humanism" to Jean Beaufret, explaining the differences between his thought and that of the French existentialists. He presented "What are Poets For?" in memory of Rilke. He renewed some old friendships, including the friendship with Arendt. He lectured on technology, language, and various philosophers. He traveled and began the preparation of a complete edition of his works, including his lectures. When complete, this will constitute about one hundred volumes.

Heidegger died on May 26, 1976. He was buried in the churchyard at Messkirch and a Catholic mass was held in his memory. His nephew served as the officiating priest.

The Call of the Pathway

In a short essay, "The Pathway," Heidegger describes a quiet path at Messkirch. In writing this description, he is also describing the call to thinking that he experienced. He writes, "The call of the pathway is now quite clear. Is it a soul speaking? Or the world? Or God?" (Sheehan 71). Heidegger's thought is best understood as a response to a call. In examining his thought, it is important to remember that the source of the call was not clear to Heidegger.

2

Dasein

While the published version of *Being and Time* was organized rather quickly, Heidegger spent many years thinking about how to structure and articulate his ideas. He presented lectures that gave indication of the direction of his thought and helped him to test and formulate important concepts. *The Genesis of Heidegger's Being and Time* by Theodore Kisiel, is an excellent study of the development of Heidegger's thought leading up to the final draft of *Being and Time*. Kisiel convincingly argues that Heidegger's breakthrough in thought that leads to *Being and Time* came in 1919 when Heidegger returned from the warfront and began working as Husserl's assistant. Heidegger developed the questions, the emphasis on the importance of hermeneutics, and some of the language that remained with him throughout his life.

When Heidegger pulled together his lecture notes and manuscript in order to produce a publication to show that he was worthy of the philosophical chair at Marburg, he planned for *Being and Time* to have two parts. Each part was to have three divisions. As published, *Being and Time* contained only the first two divisions of Part One of Heidegger's outline. While some of Heidegger's later publications can be read as the completion of the work, Heidegger never used this material to produce a revised or completed version of *Being and Time*.

For English readers of Heidegger, translation is an important issue. *Being and Time* is available in two translations. The first was done by John Macquarrie and Edward Robinson and appeared in 1962. In 1996, a new translation by Joan Stambaugh was published. Both translations can serve the English reader well and both have problems. The Macquarrie/Robinson translation is more literal and also includes more of the German so that a reader can learn some of the more important German words. The Stambaugh reads more smoothly, but some of the word choices do not help the reader understand connections between concepts that Heidegger makes. Quotations in this chapter and in Chapter 3 will be from the Macquarrie/Robinson translation. Page numbers are to the German pages. Both the Macquarrie/Robinson and the Stambaugh translations use these numbers in the margins. For concepts that are particularly important for Heidegger, German words will also be provided.

The Guiding Question

Heidegger begins *Being and Time* with a discussion of the need to retrieve the question of the meaning of Being (*Sein*). Heidegger's reading of Plato and Aristotle led him to think that the emphasis on knowledge in the philosophy of his time kept thinkers from asking the question that the Greeks had asked and which had served as the beginning for philosophical thought. He maintains that when philosophers do address this question, it is taken to have a simple answer. Being is understood as the most universal concept, as undefinable, or as self-evident and so needing no explication. Each of these approaches dismisses the need to pursue the question any further. Heidegger reviews each of these positions and concludes that "the question itself is obscure and without direction" (BT 4). Yet, if the question was important enough to serve as the beginnings for philosophical thought, there must be something to the question. Heidegger maintains that the question needs to be formulated in a way that makes sense to contemporary people. It needs to be a question that is a question for us. The rest of *Being and Time*, and perhaps the rest of Heidegger's work, can be read as an attempt to retrieve this question in such a way that we understand it as the vital question for our time. He sets out to formulate the question, not to answer it.

The Structure of Questioning

Heidegger begins to formulate the question by looking at the structure of questioning. He suggests that when we ask a question, we ask about something. In order to do this, we must already have at least some vague grasp of what we are asking about. In addition, when we ask a question we address the question to something; we interrogate someone or something. Finally, we want to find something out when we ask a question. A simple example illustrates the structure that Heidegger identifies. A friend makes the best cookies you have ever tasted. They taste so good that you want to be able to make those cookies yourself. This is what you want to find out. So, you ask your friend for the recipe. The cookies are what you ask about, and you ask the question because you already have a grasp of the cookies. The entity interrogated is your friend.

Heidegger applies this structure to the question concerning Being. What we want to know is the meaning of Being. If we are going to ask a question about Being, then Being must already be available to us in some vague way. But Being is not like a cookie. If we are going to ask about Being, we need to find a way to ask the question that recognizes the uniqueness of what we are asking about. Heidegger finds the clue as to how to begin to formulate the question in the third part of the structure of questioning, that which is interrogated. It is entities (*Seiendes*) that are questioned. We ask about the Being of entities, and each kind of entity has its own character of Being.

Ontological Difference

The distinction that Heidegger is pointing out between Being (*Sein*) and entities (*Seiendes*) is known as the ontological difference. The word "ontological" derives from the Greek word meaning being. The ontological difference is a distinction that we make everyday. Even if we are not aware of it, we draw a distinction between the fact that an entity is and the kind of entity that it is, the Being of the entity. Heidegger uses the term "ontic" to talk about entities and "ontological" to talk about Being. I am quite sure that I exist; I am aware of my everyday, ontic, existence. However, I also ask, "Who am I?" This is an ontological question. Heidegger suggests that in order to raise the question of Being in a meaningful way, we must interrogate the right

13

entity. We must figure out which entity to address. We would not ask a tree for the cookie recipe. We know that it is our friend who can provide the recipe. If we are to ask the question of the meaning of Being, we must discover which entity to question.

Heidegger determines that the inquirer is the entity to be questioned. He notes that we are each the entity that is able to ask the question of Being. This means that we have some vague, preliminary understanding of Being. If we question ourselves, we may be able to formulate the question about the meaning of Being in a more adequate way. Heidegger uses the term *"Dasein"* to name this entity that each one of us is. *"Dasein"* literally translates (t)here-being. *"Da"* can mean both "there" and "here." It is here where I am, or there where you are. In both cases, the emphasis is on the personal I or you.

The word is extremely important for Heidegger's thought. He first started using the term in 1923 after trying several other expressions. Clearly, he does not want to use terms such as human being or subject. These terms carry with them many of the presuppositions that he wants to avoid in the development of his thinking, including the dualism of much of Western thought that separates the subject from the object, the knower from that which is known. Other philosophers, especially Immanuel Kant, use the term, *Dasein*, as a philosophical term to refer to any entity. In everyday German, the word tends to be used to refer to the kind of being that belongs to persons. In selecting the everyday usage of the word rather than using a purely philosophical word, Heidegger emphasizes that we are the kinds of entities that do already have this vague understanding of Being. He says, *"Understanding of Being is itself a definite characteristic of Dasein's Being.* Dasein is ontically distinctive in that it *is* ontological" (BT 12). Heidegger makes use of the ontological difference to explain that Dasein always understands itself in terms of its existence. Each of us asks Hamlet's question, "To be or not to be?"

Questioning Dasein

After Heidegger identifies Dasein as the entity that must be questioned in order to formulate appropriately the question about the meaning of Being, he proposes that it is still necessary to find the right way to question Dasein. Heidegger notes that this may seem quite simple. We are Dasein. Ontically, in our daily existence, there is nothing closer. Yet, Heidegger says, ontologically, in terms of understanding our own Being, we are very far from ourselves. We come to understand our own Being only as we live in and construct ourselves within a world. We understand our Being as it is shown to us in the world that we help to constitute. In choosing our way in the world, we often ignore and even conceal the issue of our Being. We do not always want to know who we are. We prefer to be caught up in the day-to-day activities of our lives.

Because of this tendency, Heidegger proposes to first examine Dasein in its everydayness looking for structures that present themselves as determinative for our existence. If we can identify such structures in our everyday, ontic, lives, we may be able to reflect on these and move to an ontological level of thinking. Heidegger wants his phenomenological analysis to set this out in a way that will help all people make this ontological move, not just philosophers. His analysis of Dasein at the ontic level will be followed in this chapter. Heidegger then repeats the analysis on what he calls "a higher and authentically ontological basis" (BT 17). In this repetition, he demonstrates that temporality is the meaning of the Being of Dasein. Chapter 3 will set out this part of Heidegger's work.

The Phenomenological Method

Before beginning the analysis of Dasein, Heidegger explains in a preliminary fashion the method of phenomenology that he proposes to use in carrying out his analysis. He uses the expression that Husserl used in his early work, "To the things themselves!" But, Heidegger separates himself from Husserl in these early pages of *Being and Time*. In helping Heidegger with page proofs, Husserl did not fully understand this break. Later, when he really read the opening sections of *Being and Time* more carefully, Husserl understood that Heidegger had taken phenomenology in a direction far different from his own.

Heidegger emphasizes that phenomenology is not like other studies that are termed "-ologies." Theology is the study of God. Psychology is the study of the human psyche. Each of these terms tells us <u>what</u> is to be studied. Heidegger says that phenomenology is concerned with <u>how</u> the thing is approached. Phenomenology as an approach lets us see by helping to uncover what is hidden or concealed. Phenomenology resists imposing a structure of understanding. Rather, it tries to let things reveal themselves. Heidegger develops phenomenology as an approach to understanding that does not assume

15

that understanding requires a subject to stand over against an object of understanding. Indeed, Heidegger believes that this dualistic approach to understanding only further serves to conceal and cover over. If the question of the meaning of Being is to be formulated appropriately, it must be done in such a way that Being can show itself. Meaning must not be imposed.

Heidegger says that the phenomenology of Dasein is hermeneutics. He later acknowledges his debt to Friedrich Schleiermacher for this term. While he does not emphasize the term in *Being and Time* or in his later writings, the step that he takes in using this term is perhaps the most important part of all of Heidegger's philosophy. Traditionally, hermeneutics is the art of interpretation. Usually it refers to interpretation of texts. There are legal hermeneutics, literary hermeneutics, and religious hermeneutics. All can be understood as theories or ways of interpretation. Schleiermacher broadened hermeneutics, trying to set out the art of interpretation in general. Clearly, in all of these types of hermeneutics, one of the main purposes of understanding is to make meaning clear, to take a text and let it speak truthfully. Schleiermacher emphasizes the importance of the art of listening for hermeneutics. If a text is to be allowed to speak, the human art is an art of listening.

Heidegger takes these insights and broadens hermeneutics even further. Hermeneutics is the interpretation of Dasein's Being. Phenomenology as hermeneutics is the process of self-understanding that is possible for Dasein. Dasein is the kind of entity that interprets. This is how Dasein is able to know itself and so uncover its own Being. At one level, what Heidegger is suggesting is easily understood. We come to understand ourselves in the process of understanding the world in which we live. Children begin to understand the world by developing words and concepts. In understanding the world in this way, children also begin to develop a self-understanding. Children can speak, conceptualize, and understand. They also recognize the emergence of these processes. Children become excited when they learn new words and when they make conceptual leaps. Heidegger pushes this insight. By examining how we understand ourselves, we will have a better understanding of who we are in the most fundamental sense. We will be able to understand the kind of Being that is Dasein's Being.

Heidegger emphasizes that it is already apparent that when Dasein seeks to understand itself, it is not looking for its essence. Dasein is not trying to understand itself in the same way that it understands a chair. In understanding a chair, we define the properties that something must have in order to be a chair. For example, a chair is defined as having a seat. Dasein does not seek to define its own properties. Rather, Dasein seeks to understand the possibilities of its existence. Heidegger says that phenomenology will set out the existential structure of Dasein, not Dasein's properties or categories.

Being-In-The-World (*In-der-Welt-sein*)

Dasein is that entity of which each of us must say, "I am that entity." Heidegger maintains that an analysis of Dasein, must begin with the understanding that Dasein's basic state is that of Being-in-the-world. Heidegger uses the hyphenated word to emphasize that Dasein does not begin as separate from the world or from other entities in the world and then piece together a world. Dasein is always already in the world and is a part of that world. It is where we live. Heidegger's point is in many respects quite simple, yet it is often overlooked both in philosophy and in our everyday life. We do not have a position from outside of the world from which we can understand the world. Nor are we in the world in such a way that we are distant from the things in the world.

Heidegger develops the insight that we experience ourselves as always already situated in our world. Being-in-the-world is not a property that we have. We cannot escape this aspect of our existence. Moreover, we are absorbed in this world. For example, when we gather at a table for a family meal or a meal with friends, we engage in conversation. The chairs, the table, even the food, are there as part of the world of the evening. We use the things, but we do not focus on those things. If the conversation needs an example, they may suddenly emerge into our direct awareness. However, our immediate relationship with these things is closeness. We are in the world in such a way that we touch things in our world and they touch us. We recognize that we are bound together with the entities of our world. We can meet and understand entities only as they are available in our world. The world is where we encounter everything that is.

Heidegger's phenomenological analysis of Being-in-the-world is recognized as one of the most powerful examples of phenomenological description. Its richness is part of what makes *Being and Time* such an important philosophical work. No one summary or reading can do it justice. This reading focuses on Heidegger's insights into the importance of recognizing that Dasein is a situated and relational being.

An analysis of our everydayness shows us that we do not exist in independence from what we encounter in the world. Heidegger's analysis focuses on our encounters with entities that do not have the character of Dasein, with entities that do have this character, and with our encounter with Dasein as the entity that each of us is. While each of these aspects of world can be examined separately, it should be remembered that no part ever exists in separation from the other parts. Being-in-the-world is a unity.

Encountering Things

Heidegger characterizes the way in which we encounter things in the world as circumspective concern (*Besorge*). We do not come to know things from an objective distance. We always encounter things in the world in an involved manner. In describing how we encounter things, Heidegger makes an interesting and helpful distinction between things that are handy (*Zuhandenes*) and things that are on-hand or present-at-hand (*Vorhandenes*).

We can encounter things in the world as present-at-hand. We can distance ourselves from the things and approach them theoretically. This is how philosophers usually approach things and the world. Descartes, for example, began his philosophical thought by completely doubting his connection with the world. After long internal analysis, he restores the world. But this world is one of mathematical physics. Things are all known as extended things to be measured. While this way of encountering things in the world does enable us to live in the world, it does not disclose the most fundamental way that we encounter things in the world. In fact, this approach to the world serves to further conceal Dasein's primary way of being-in-the world.

Heidegger maintains that the more fundamental way in which we encounter things is as handy. Things are disclosed in our use of them. Heidegger uses the example of a hammer. When we use a hammer to pound a nail, we do not think about the lever structure that is at work in the hammer. We use the hammer in a very practical way. We use it to pound the nail into the wall so that we can hang the picture. We do not deal with the hammer by staring at it and contemplating it. We manipulate and use the hammer. But we do gain a type of knowledge in this relationship with the hammer. We learn how to pound nails, and so learn what the thing is for. The hammer is disclosed in the context of its useful relationship to us.

Learning to ride a bicycle may be a more helpful example for contemporary readers. When a person learns to ride, someone else, often a parent, may offer all kinds of advice as to what to do. But the real task is to develop a handy relationship with the bicycle. Rather than think about how to gain balance, how to pedal, and how to stop, learning to ride a bicycle is the task of encountering the bike in such a close relationship that no "thinking" is required. Indeed, anyone who has learned to ride a bicycle has probably had the experience of suddenly starting to think about how to do one of these things and breaking the close relationship with the bike in a fall.

Most of our everyday encounters with things in the world are of the things as handy, in our practical relationships with the things. But this does not mean that we do not know the things. We do know what the hammer is for. Carpenters and others experienced in building know how the hammer is situated in relationship to all kinds of other tools used in construction. Once a person has learned to ride a bicycle, that person can give recommendations to another person about how to ride. Heidegger says that that we have circumspective knowledge. We have an awareness of how the things fit within the world in which we live. Depending on the nature of our concernful absorption in the world, things are disclosed in different ways. The work that we do makes it possible for us to know things and provides the perspective from which we know things.

Heidegger's analysis moves from this recognition that Dasein primarily encounters things in the world as handy, to a further description of how Dasein is situated in the world. To be situated does not mean to be in a space like a thing that is present-at-hand. Nor does it mean to be handy, available for Dasein's use. Dasein's world is spatial, but not in the way that Descartes defines it. Dasein is situated such that it deals with these entities "concernfully and with familiarity" (BT 104). Heidegger says that Dasein's spatiality is characterized by bringing things close and giving them directionality. The world in which Dasein lives is characterized by up and down, right and left. Insofar as Dasein is, it already has its place, its "own discovered region" (BT 108). Dasein is spatial in that it opens a realm of concern in which Dasein is involved with things.

Spatiality is a fundamental way in which we are in the world. But this means that we belong in our world. We are always involved and engaged. We are able to open our world, or make it larger, by involving ourselves with more things and by relating to these things so that they can show us possibilities of how we can be related to them. It is worth noting that just because Heidegger characterizes Dasein's

19

relationship to things with the term concern, does not mean that our concern always results in positive outcomes for entities in the world.

Encountering Others

Heidegger begins his interpretation of Dasein by focusing on things in the world, especially as they are handy, in order to emphasize that Dasein is absorbed in the world, not distant from it. In describing how Dasein encounters others, he takes a similar approach. While he emphasizes that Dasein is in each case mine, he also suggests that this can be misleading. Dasein is not an isolated self, but is always absorbed in relationship with others. Just as he emphasizes that things are not extended entities separate from me, occupying space and time, so too he emphasizes that others are not simply every other person. Others are those with whom I share the world. Dasein's Being is a being-with. Even when alone, Dasein's way of being-in-the-world is being-with, it is intimately connected to others.

Heidegger uses the word concern (*Besorge*) to describe Dasein's way of relating to things in the world. He uses solicitude (*Fürsorge*) to describe Dasein's way of relating to others in the world. He says that our relationship with others is usually based on a common concern. We are engaged together in common tasks. In these activities we express solicitude towards others. We are concerned about the welfare of the other. This solicitude can include being against another as much as being for the other. Even when one is for the other, solicitude can be expressed in extremely different ways.

For example, a parent can desire success for a child in a little league baseball game. The parent is for the child and behaves in a way that clearly demonstrates that the parent takes the welfare of the child to be of central importance. The parent can take over for the child. Anyone who has ever participated in this sport has seen this happen. The parent argues with the coach or with the referee about the child. The parent can also simply attend the games and cheer the child on, while letting the child make mistakes and achieve successes. Both parents are expressing solicitude.

Heidegger maintains that Dasein not only encounters others in the world, Dasein is absorbed in the world of these others. He says we are absorbed in the "they." He describes this absorption,

This   Being-with-one-another   dissolves   one's   own   Dasein

20

completely into the kind of Being of 'the Others', in such a way, indeed, that the Others, as distinguishable and explicit, vanish more and more. In this inconspicuousness and unascertainability, the real dictatorship of the "they" is unfolded. We take pleasure and enjoy ourselves as <u>they</u> take pleasure; we read, see, and judge about literature and art as <u>they</u> see and judge; likewise we shrink back from the 'great mass' as <u>they</u> shrink back; we find 'shocking' what <u>they</u> find shocking. (BT 126-27)

We experience and know the world in terms of the average ways that are determined by and with others. The "they" constitutes a leveling and a limiting of Dasein. We become absorbed in idle chatter or gossip. Our curiosity is shaped by what captivates the public. To understand itself authentically, Dasein must disclose what is concealed in average everyday understanding.

Heidegger can be read as an existentialist at this point. He uses language that indicates that the authentic Dasein will be an individual Dasein that breaks from the "they" and formulates an authentic identity. Yet, it also seems appropriate to read Heidegger as showing us that we are always born into a community and our understandings, tastes, and opinions are formed within that community. Because we live in this way, we all tend to lose sight of the fundamental issue of who we are. We lose sight of what it is to be human in the process of daily living. The call to authenticity is not simply a call to individual authenticity. It is also a call to humans in community. To be human is to recognize the need to discover how this "they-self" functions to conceal what it is to be Dasein.

Encountering Dasein

Heidegger takes another major step in his description by setting out what he takes to be the existential constitution of Dasein. Again, he emphasizes that he is not describing properties or characteristics of a human. He is describing fundamental structures of existence. He proposes to disclose what remains hidden in our average everyday lives. He describes the fundamental way in which Dasein, each one of us, exists in the world. Previous philosophers have suggested a number of ways of defining what is fundamental about human existence. Humans are rational animals, religious beings, thinking things. Phenomenology aims to let Dasein reveal itself, interpret itself.

Heidegger suggests that disposition, understanding, interpretation, and language are all fundamental and interrelated structures of our existence. Each of these helps disclose Dasein and so helps us encounter Dasein, that is encounter ourselves.

Heidegger begins his description with the claim that Dasein is always in a disposition or mood (*Befindlichkeit*). While we can change or alter our disposition or mood, we cannot be without one. This is a total orientation towards the world, a pervasive disposition. We say that we are well-disposed towards the day or we are in a bad mood. We find ourselves in a mood. We are just in a mood. Because we are in a mood, we experience our world in certain ways. For example, if we are fearful, we can discover what is threatening in the world or we can experience the world as threatening. Our disposition is always the starting point for how we understand.

Reflecting on the fact that we are always in a disposition shows us that we are "thrown" into the world. We do not have total control over ourselves. But we are also always in the situation of understanding (*Verstehen*) the world, entities in the world, and ourselves. Heidegger says that in understanding, Dasein projects itself. Heidegger is constantly playing with language. In this case, the play of language also works well in English. If we are thrown into the world, we also throw ourselves into the world. When we understand, we show ourselves our own possibilities. Out of a fearful disposition, we project possibilities for ourselves. We do not simply respond to the world. We lock our homes, set alarms, and purchase weapons. In projecting possibilities, Dasein discloses how it is in the world. It interprets itself.

Heidegger says, "In interpretation, understanding does not become something different. It becomes itself" (BT 148). In interpretation (*Auslegung*), we disclose how we are involved with the world. We interpret something as something. For example, out of a fearful disposition, I project possibilities of threat. I understand my neighbor as a danger. Heidegger describes what is known as the fore-structure of understanding. He says that when we interpret what we understand, we already have it. We cannot understand something, if we do not have some vague everyday relationship with it. Heidegger calls this fore-having. In addition, understanding is always from a point of view. This is fore-sight. Finally, understanding always takes place in terms of concepts that we use. This is fore-conception. In the case of the neighbor that I understand as a danger, I must first have a neighbor. Out of my fearful disposition, I approach my neighbor from a fearful way of seeing, and so I use concepts like "dangerous" to express my understanding. In this process I establish a relationship with my neighbor. Heidegger says Dasein appropriates what is understood.

Two insights into the existential structure of Dasein emerge from the description of the fore-structure of understanding. Understanding is never without presuppositions. We do not, and cannot, understand anything from a purely objective position. We always understand from within the context of our disposition and involvement in the world. In addition, it is clear that understanding always involves language (*Sprache*). We are speaking beings. If understanding is a projection of possibilities, this projection takes place fundamentally in language. Heidegger's later work will focus more directly on language, especially poetry.

In *Being and Time*, Heidegger returns to examine aspects of everyday existence in light of the description of Dasein's existential structure. He looks at idle chatter and curiosity. He says,

> *Idle talk discloses to Dasein a Being towards the world, towards Others, and towards itself - a Being in which these are understood, but in a mode of groundless floating. Curiosity discloses everything and anything, yet in such a way that Being-in is everywhere and nowhere.* (BT 177)

Heidegger returns to the point that he made at the beginning of his analysis. Dasein loses itself in the "they." We gossip and gawk, not to understand, but simply for the sake of chatter and idle curiosity. We do not try to seriously understand ourselves. Heidegger describes this basic state of Dasein as falling. While this term has many theological implications that Heidegger wants to avoid, he still thinks it is an appropriate term for describing Dasein's situation. We are in the world in a kind of turbulence, always losing ourselves. We get entangled in the world and sucked into the averageness of the "they." In the process, we conceal the possibilities that are ours.

Care (*Sorge*)

Heidegger's description of being-in-the world takes a lengthy path. He describes human finitude beginning with the insight that we get lost in our everyday lives, the ontic, and so forget or are oblivious to our Being, the ontological. In the course of the analysis of being-in-the-world, we get glimpses of the ontological, but we also recognize that these glimpses are quickly concealed in our daily activities. For example, we may recognize that our relationship with our neighbor is based on presuppositions. Recognizing this fact places us in a better position to examine those presuppositions and ask what attitude toward our neighbor would best help us to know the neighbor. However, at the moment when the neighbor appears, the unreflective attitudes suddenly emerge and we again meet the neighbor with suspicion. The task that Heidegger has set for Dasein is to understand itself. In order to do this Dasein must somehow overcome this entanglement in the everyday. Yet, Dasein cannot withdraw from its ontic reality. What it must do is regain sight of the ontological without leaving its everyday existence.

Heidegger selects the disposition of anxiety as particularly helpful for trying to grasp Dasein in an ontological and total way. His selects anxiety as particularly helpful because it "brings Dasein back from its falling, and makes manifest to it that authenticity and inauthenticity are possibilities of its Being" (BT 191). When we are anxious, we are forced to face ourselves. Heidegger is not talking about a particular fear, but about those occasions when we are taken over by a total anxiety. In those moments, we come face to face with ourselves. We cannot hide in the "they." Heidegger calls the totality structure that is disclosed to Dasein in anxiety, "care."

Heidegger uses "care" to give expression to Dasein's total relational way of being-in-the-world. To care is both to acknowledge that something matters and to care for something, to clearly act on the recognition that something matters. Heidegger says that it is because our basic way of being-in-the-world is care (*Sorge*) that we can have concern (*Besorge*) for entities in the world and solicitude (*Fürsorge*) for others. Heidegger describes the structure of care as "Being-ahead-of-oneself -- in-Being-already-in... -- as Being-alongside" (BT 196). He admits that this description may seem strange. But what Heidegger is attempting to articulate is that Dasein always exists in such a way that it is directed towards something. While Dasein finds itself thrown into a world, Dasein projects possibilities for itself and so is ahead of itself. At the same time, Dasein is with others in the world and along-side entities that are handy. Care is used to give expression to this complex web of relations that is characteristic of Dasein's way of being-in-the-world. Care shows us that the Being of Dasein is not simple.

Disclosedness (*Erschlossenheit*)

In *Being and Time*, Heidegger proposes to move from the articulation of the fundamental structure of Dasein as care to a further analysis of this totality that is characterized by temporality. First, however, he includes a section on the relation of Dasein to truth. Heidegger's work on truth will be explored more fully in Chapter 4. However, it is important for understanding *Being and Time* to note that Heidegger connects truth to what he calls Dasein's disclosedness.

If Dasein's basic way of being-in-the-world is relational, then previous philosophical understandings of truth are inadequate. These all begin by giving priority to Dasein's relation to the present-at-hand. They treat human knowing as the overcoming of distance between a subject and an object. But Heidegger has show that Dasein's basic way of relating to entities in the world is to experience things as handy, as useful, and to be-with others. In doing this, Dasein discloses. Dasein's way of being in the world is one of opening up possibilities, of uncovering things. Dasein always understands things from a perspective and so entities are always understood as something. Things are not understood in terms of some unchangeable essence. Things are always understood in a context.

Heidegger says that disclosedness belongs to Dasein's state of Being. As such, Dasein can be in the truth or in untruth. Dasein can open up a world in which entities can reveal themselves to Dasein. But Dasein can also open the world in such a way as to prevent this revelation. Dasein's projection of possibilities can cover things up.

This insight becomes more important for Heidegger's later philosophy, especially for his work on language. In *Being and Time*, Heidegger returns to his task of giving a phenomenological description of Dasein that will more adequately characterize the unity of Dasein's being-in-the-world and its ontological implications. Heidegger turns to a description of Dasein's temporality. If Dasein is to open a space in which the question of the meaning of Being can be asked in such a way that Being can be disclosed, Dasein must have a yet more ontological understanding of itself.

3

Temporality

In the second division of *Being and Time*, Heidegger proposes to set out the ontological meaning of care as temporality. Heidegger shows that Dasein's being is best understood as temporality. When reading Heidegger, temporality should not be understood in a chronological sense. Rather, temporality is the movement of Dasein's becoming. This means that we are always moving towards our future. In doing this, we are becoming who we are. We become present to ourselves. The temporality that is fundamental to Dasein shows us our finitude.

Heidegger suggests that the first division of *Being and Time* develops a description of Dasein that is based on only a partial "having" of Dasein. The explication of care as the structure of Dasein's being serves only as a preliminary description. The first part of the analysis has focused primarily on Dasein's everydayness and on aspects of Dasein such as particular dispositions or moods. The task that remains is to grasp Dasein as a whole and as authentic. Heidegger proposes to develop on to a description of Dasein that will disclose Dasein in its authentic totality. Heidegger focuses on death in order to understand Dasein in its totality. He focuses on conscience in order to understand Dasein's authenticity.

Death

Heidegger says that death limits and determines Dasein's possibilities. If Dasein is to be grasped in its totality, death must be included. If we are to understand ourselves, we must grasp our mortality. But as long as Dasein is, death is still outside of or beyond it. As long as we are alive, we are projecting possibilities for ourselves. Even though we are aware that we are mortal, or at least become aware of this the older we become, we continue to think of the future. We plan what we will do this afternoon, tomorrow, next week, and next year. As Heidegger has pointed out, we are always ahead of ourselves. If Heidegger's analysis is to continue, there must be a way for Dasein to grasp its death.

One possibility is that Dasein can experience the death of others. Certainly much can be learned by observing the death of another person. When we watch another person die, we observe a transition from one kind of being to another. In Heidegger's language, we can observe an entity change from a Dasein to an entity present-at-hand. But we can never experience another's death. Heidegger emphasizes that Dasein is each of us. The analysis of Dasein is something that we can and must each do ourselves. If Dasein is to be grasped and examined in its totality, we must each be able to grasp our own death. Heidegger believes that we can do this. He does not mean that we can each know the time and nature of our deaths. But we can and do exist as being-towards-death. We understand our mortality.

In our everyday lives death is usually concealed. Contemporary practices in relation to death exemplify this. We seldom say that someone died. Instead, we say that a person "passed" or indicate that the person has gone somewhere such as heaven, or to be with God or someone who has died before them. We also assure people, even those that we know are dying, that they have a long time to live. Heidegger says that in our everyday lives, absorbed as we are in the "they," we flee from death. But this very fleeing reveals our understanding that death is certain and indefinite. We know that we will die, and we know that when we will die is not definite. We also know that we will die alone. Heidegger writes, "death, as the end of Dasein, is Dasein's ownmost possibility – non-relational, certain and as such indefinite, not to be outstripped" (BT 258-59).

Heidegger points out that even as we develop social structures that help us conceal and flee from death, we reveal our deepest understanding that we are mortal. Death can help us to grasp ourselves as a totality, if we accept death as our ownmost possibility. This does not mean that we should brood over death and despair. Nor does it mean that we should try to hasten death as we might other possibilities that we project for ourselves. If we anticipate death, we face ourselves authentically. Heidegger says that we can then live our lives with a "freedom towards death" (BT 266). This freedom does not release us from our finitude and mortality, but it does release us from the illusions that take place in the "they." We understand that we have been lost in the "they" and that we can find ourselves.

This freedom is sometimes seen in people who have had near-death experiences or who have been deeply touched by the death of someone else. As they recognize their own mortality, they are freed to enjoy the present. They may try things they have never tried before. They may give opinions that earlier they would have held back because they were too caught up in what others would think. We say that they have accepted death. But this acceptance does make them morbid or depressed. In the light of death, each moment is valued and each decision is viewed in its appropriate significance. Heidegger says, in this freedom, Dasein can hear the call of conscience.

Conscience

Conscience, according to Heidegger, is this awakened awareness of our finite, moral existence. He says that when we are absorbed in the "they," we listen to idle talk and to the leveling chatter that goes on. What we fail to hear is ourselves. The call of conscience breaks through this hubbub. It does not participate in the chatter, but silently asks us to face who we are. Heidegger says it calls us forth to our possibilities (BT 274).

The call of conscience should not be understood as coming from some power beyond or outside of Dasein. Heidegger does not want the call to be understood as the call of God or of anything that transcends human finitude. He writes,

> *Conscience manifests itself as the call of care: the caller is Dasein, which, in its thrownness is anxious about its potentiality-for-Being. The one to whom the appeal is made is this very same Dasein, summoned to its ownmost potentiality-for-Being. Dasein is falling into the "they," and it is summoned out of this falling by the appeal. (BT 277)*

28

Conscience calls us to be true to ourselves.

Heidegger says that the voice of conscience speaks to us of our guilt. Again, Heidegger uses words that are filled with religious, especially Christian, signification and that can sometimes be misleading. Guilt should not be understood here as any particular moral fault. The call of conscience does not say we are guilty because we continue eating the snack food, or even because we have harmed another person. Our guilt is our incompleteness. What we are guilty of is a refusal to acknowledge our own finitude. We can refuse the call of conscience and be inauthentic. This means that we remain in the "they," hiding from the reality of our mortality. Or, we can respond to the call of conscience and become authentic.

Heidegger calls the response to the call of conscience, resoluteness (*Entschlossenheit*). He says that it is a distinctive mode of Dasein's disclosedness (*Erschlossenheit*). In responding to the call of conscience, Dasein determines to be true to itself. This means living in such a way as to disclose things, others, and itself while also acknowledging the fundamental finitude of Dasein.

Temporality and Finitude

Having examined death and conscience, Heidegger returns to the concern with which he began the second division of *Being and Time*. He develops a description that will enable us to grasp Dasein in its totality. At the end of the first division, care came close to providing this unity. At that point Heidegger defined care as "ahead-of-itself-already-being-in (a world) as Being-alongside (entities encountered within-the-world)" (BT 327). The examinations of death and conscience have led to resoluteness. Heidegger points out that resoluteness shows us a "unity of a future which makes present in the process of having been" (BT 326). Both of these concepts are defined in terms of a relational structure that exhibits what may be generally taken as a future, past, and present. Heidegger says that the unity that was apparent in care and that is again disclosed in resoluteness is most appropriately understood as temporality.

Both care and resoluteness show Dasein's basic structure as threefold temporality. While Heidegger's analysis includes complexities that are philosophically important, his description is at one level quite easily understood. To be human is to be directed towards the future, to always be becoming oneself. However, in

29

moving into the future, our past is always with us. This past is both our individual past and the historical past that has helped form our pre-understandings. In this process of becoming what we already are, we are present. We disclose ourselves to ourselves and others and we disclose things in their present, situated, relationship to us. This entire process is temporality. Because of this, Dasein's present, and so all meaning that is disclosed, is always finite. It is incomplete and in the process of becoming.

Heidegger is, however, hesitant to simply use the language of future, present, and past. These terms carry many presuppositions that Heidegger is trying to get us to overcome and think beyond. In developing the concept of temporality, Heidegger develops what he terms the "ecstases" of temporality (BT 329). This way of articulating temporality was developed in 1926, shortly before the finalization of the published version of *Being and Time*. Heidegger's selection of this term is intended to make the connection between existence and temporality more evident and emphasizes the process nature of temporality. We have a tendency to understand time in terms of a series of spatial points. Heidegger sets out an understanding of temporality that helps us understand our finitude from the position of our lived experience.

Heidegger calls on his early university studies to illustrate how different the understanding of temporality that he is developing is from earlier understandings. He notes that from the position of Newtonian physics, it is not possible to understand quantum physics. Only when one enters into the conceptual framework of quantum physics can both types of physics be understood appropriately. The implication is that the conception of temporality that Heidegger is articulating is more fundamental than other conceptions of time. Heidegger calls the type of temporality that he is describing "primordial time." If we can understand temporality as ecstatic, we can have a better understanding of all of the ways that we understand time.

In selecting the term "ecstases," Heidegger is pointing out the manner in which our existence is always outside of itself. This does not mean that we are first some substance or self that then moves outside of itself. Rather, it means that our existence always has a direction. We are always oriented towards our possibilities, towards the past as it is part of our existence, and towards entities in the world of our existence. While these moments are differentiated, they also constitute a unified whole. This is temporality.

It seems that Heidegger has in some ways completed his analysis. He began with the concern of how to ask the question of the meaning of Being. It is now clear that that question can only be formulated from within the structure of Dasein's temporality.   However, Heidegger emphasizes the importance of everydayness. He says,

> *We must reveal everydayness in its temporal meaning, so that the problematic included in temporality may come to light, and the seeming 'obvious' character of the preparatory analyses may completely disappear.* (BT 332)

Heidegger's analysis returns to the everydayness with which it began.

Temporality and Everydayness

Heidegger returns to understanding, disposition, falling and discourse.   He shows that each of these structures of Dasein's everydayness gives priority to a certain ecstasis. Understanding orients Dasein towards its possibilities. In understanding we recognize our focus on the future, on becoming.   Disposition discloses Dasein's orientation towards the past, towards what we already are.   Falling discloses Dasein's orientation towards the present. Heidegger develops examples that show that while each of these structures of Dasein's everydayness exhibits a primary ecstasis, we also come up against the whole of temporality in each of these structures.   Heidegger is demonstrating that in each aspect of the everyday structure of Dasein, the unity of temporality is evident.

His discussion of falling is particularly helpful in order to understand his analysis. Falling is the term that Heidegger uses to describe the entanglement of Dasein in the superficialness of the "they." In the first part of *Being and Time*, he used idle talk, curiosity, and ambiguity to illustrate this aspect of Dasein. When he returns to this aspect of Dasein's everydayness, he focuses on the example of curiosity. He shows that while curiosity shows Dasein as absorbed in the present, it also illustrates the unity of temporality.

Heidegger is talking about the sort of curiosity that leads us to want to slow down at the scene of an accident and stare. We do not want to understand anything about the accident. Heidegger says of such a situation that we seek "to see only in order to see and to have seen" (BT 346). We are focused on the present. We stare and gawk. Yet, we quickly move on. We look on down the road for what is coming next. While this is inauthentic, it is futural. We crave another

31

experience to give us something to talk about. In moving away from one experience and craving another, we indicate that we have already had an experience. The contemporary expression "Been there, done that!" exemplifies this type of inauthentic existence. We are constantly in search of new experiences because we are focused on the pleasure or excitement of the moment. At first this seems to mean that we live only in the present, but both our actions and our language reveal all three ecstases of temporality. Even in our most thoroughly inauthentic everydayness, we are temporal.

It is worth asking why Heidegger returns to a discussion of Dasein's everydayness. He has moved from Dasein's everyday, inauthentic, existence to an analysis of the ontological structure that makes it possible for Dasein to be authentic. Since it would seem that we would want to be authentic, it would also seem that we would want to avoid returning to everydayness and its fascination with the "they."

Heidegger is persistent in his insistence that Dasein exists in everydayness. Just because we have a grasp of the ecstatic structure of our existence does not mean that we do not become absorbed in our daily activities. Someone who has become resolute still needs to prepare food, still becomes absorbed in the working of the equipment that is used in daily activity. Even the most resolute person will find him or herself staring at the traffic accident. Heidegger writes, "'Everydayness' manifestly stands for that way of existing in which Dasein maintains itself 'everyday'" (BT 370). Dasein is dominated by life and by the how of living life. We live in a world with others and with the tasks of our daily lives. Even when we try not to be absorbed in the everyday, it is still determinative for our lives. Heidegger says, "In the moment of vision, indeed, and often just 'for that moment,' existence can even gain the mastery over the "everyday:" but it can never extinguish it" (BT 371).

Historicality (*Geschichtlichkeit*)

Again, it may seem that Heidegger's thought is at a point where it could stop. He has set out the unitary structure of Dasein as temporality, has explained authentic existence, and has shown that even in the face of authentic existence, to be finite is to remain in the everyday and so slip back into inauthenticity. However, Heidegger recognizes a further problem for any explication that hopes to set out the being of Dasein. If Heidegger's analysis of Dasein is complicated by the persistence of inauthentic everydayness, historicality adds yet another twist to Dasein's existence.

In arriving at temporality as the unity of Dasein, Heidegger relied on the understanding that Dasein as a being that is oriented towards an end. The end that he focused on was death, and so he focused on the primacy of the future for Dasein. Dasein is always already ahead of itself. We are always projecting possibilities and concerned with what lies ahead. But Dasein stretches out between two ends. That other end is Dasein's birth or beginning. Just as we need to grasp death in order to understand our totality, we must also grasp birth.

Heidegger is not suggesting that the biological event of birth is what needs to be grasped. Birth is our beginning. If death is something which is an isolated event for each individual, Heidegger recognizes that birth takes place in a social setting. We do not come into the world by ourselves. We are brought into the world in the context of a community. We are always already with others. Heidegger emphasizes that the past is always part of us, present in us, as a living tradition. If death brings us face-to-face with the finitude that we must each accept, birth discloses the communal nature of our finitude. We exist historically.

Interpretations of Heidegger that situate him primarily within existentialist philosophy because of his focus on death and use of the language of existence often overlook Heidegger's emphasis on the communal. He writes,

> But if fateful Dasein, as Being-in-the-world, exists essentially in Being-with-Others, its historizing is a co-historizing and is determinative for it as destiny [Geschick]. This is how we designate the historizing of the community, of a people. (BT 384)

In developing the importance of historicality for the analysis of Dasein, Heidegger uses a number of German words that are related to *geschehen*, which means to happen or occur. Heidegger is using these words to emphasize that the past is entwined with our present existence.

Our past is not culture separated from those who lived in the past. We are part of communities that embody traditions. In tradition, what is past is handed over. Heidegger says that we repeat possibilities of existence that have been handed down to us. This repetition is not going back to the past and experiencing as those who lived then experienced it, nor is it bringing the past into our present in some unchanged fashion. Repetition is projecting the possibility of the past as a possibility for our own existence. Heidegger says that "Repetition does not abandon itself to that which is past, nor does it aim at progress" (BT 386). Repetition discloses Dasein's history as open.

The example of marriage, while not an example that Heidegger uses, illustrates his point. We are born into a world in which our community has a tradition of marriage. Insofar as we continue to participate in marriages, each one of us explicitly hands on this tradition. We take the tradition as a living possibility for ourselves. In embracing a particular marriage as the possibility for my life, I understand the heritage that is mine. It becomes a living heritage. But embracing this possibility is also the activity of the community. In the marriage ceremony, a possibility for the entire community is disclosed. In a Quaker marriage, for example, many of the guests rise to speak. They may speak of the two people who are marrying, or of the event of marriage, or of their own marriage. In any case, the marriage becomes an explicit act of handing on the past.

As Heidegger has demonstrated, Dasein's tendency to become lost in the "they" can result in Dasein trying to avoid death by concealing it. In a similar manner, Dasein can also flee from the past. When this happens, the past becomes unrecognizable. Heidegger writes, "When, however, one's existence is inauthentically historical, it is loaded down with the legacy of a 'past' which has become unrecognizable, and it seeks the modern (BT 391). Distinguishing authentic historical existence from inauthentic historical existence, especially within a community, is a difficult task.

The marriage example can again illustrate this point. Perhaps those who are marrying are simply caught up in the "they." They are caught up in the idle chatter that surrounds romantic love. The marriage is not a repetition in that it does not explicitly hand on a tradition. Those witnessing the marriage can also be caught up in simply being there and being seen. They are not brought to an awareness of the heritage and meaning of marriage. It is also possible that being caught up in the "they," in the social pressure to marry, individuals and the community can come to overlook or conceal the inauthentic aspects of the social institution itself. They end up perpetuating social practices that keep individuals from being authentic and that also keep communities from authentic traditions.

Heidegger notes that this concept of historicality gives indication of the need for rethinking historiology as a science. He develops the beginning of a critique of the methodology of contemporary historians, but more importantly for his own future thinking, he shows the need for philosophy to rethink what it means to reflect on the history of philosophy. Heidegger maintains that thinkers need to retrieve the history of philosophy. This means that the questions asked and the insights gained by the previous philosophers, especially the Greeks, need to be brought forward. But in retrieving this work, philosophers must be constantly aware of the tendency of finite human existence to conceal and cover over. The task of authentic philosophy is to bring the tradition of philosophy forward into a living discussion with the present. Much of Heidegger's further philosophical work focuses on this task

On the Way

Heidegger ends *Being and Time* by giving a sense of the incompleteness of the task that he set for himself. He gives a further account of the relation of temporality to everyday concepts of time, but concludes with questions about the relation of time to Being. He does not propose to have given the reader an answer. What he has provided is the beginnings of a way. He says that the way he has set out is only one possible way that can be taken. He writes of this way,

> One must seek a *way* of casting light on the fundamental question of ontology, and this is the way one must *go*. Whether this is the *only* way or even the right one at all, can be decided only *after one has gone along it*. (BT 437)

The way that Heidegger opened excited the young philosophers of his time and continues to challenge much of contemporary philosophy. While Heidegger never completed *Being and Time* as planned, the rest of his thinking continues to develop and open the directions that he sets in this work.

4

Truth

Some readers of Heidegger find a dramatic shift in his thinking after the publication of *Being and Time*. They even speak of Heidegger I and Heidegger II. Beginning in about 1930, Heidegger's work does shift style and, to some extent, topics. He uses the word turn (*Kehre*) of his own thinking. His use of the term is not primarily intended to point out a change of style and certainly does not indicate that he changed his mind about the analysis carried out in *Being and Time*. The turn that he speaks of is best understood as a thinking that begins from the analysis of *Being and Time*.

The analysis of Dasein challenges contemporary human self-understanding. We tend to believe that we are subjects that can come to objective knowledge about objects. Heidegger challenges the claim that knowledge can be without presuppositions. His analysis discloses human existence as fundamentally relational. We are in the world, and while we project our possibilities on that world, we are also thrown into the world. Moreover, we are in the world in such a way that we disclose entities and ourselves. We might say that we experience ourselves as claimed or pulled in a process of coming to know. We do not experience ourselves as uninvolved objective knowers.

The analysis of Dasein in *Being and Time* positions the philosopher as a finite being within the world. The philosopher cannot take a position above or outside of human existence. This positioning requires the philosopher to raise questions in a fundamentally different way than has been standard philosophical practice. The task of

36

philosophy is to begin thinking from a position that is finite and that must acknowledge its presuppositional structure. In a note appended to the essay, "On the Essence of Truth," Heidegger writes, "The course of the questioning is intrinsically the way of a thinking which, instead of furnishing representations and concepts, experiences and tries itself as a transformation of its relatedness to Being" (BW 141). Much of Heidegger's later work is a "trying" of thinking. This chapter and those to follow will examine the direction that Heidegger's thinking takes on a number of topics that are important for philosophical thought. Truth, art, humanism, language, and technology will be explored. These chapters do not cover all of Heidegger's work. They are intended to provide a general basic introduction. In order to begin to understand Heidegger's thought, the process of the thought is as, or more, important than the concepts. The chapters that follow will emphasize that process. Many of the essays that provide the focus for this introduction are printed in *Basic Writings*, edited by David Farrell Krell. Where possible, references will be to the translations included in that anthology.

The Essence of Truth

As noted in Chapter 2, Heidegger recognizes that the analysis of Dasein has serious implications for a concept of truth. In *Being and Time*, Heidegger connects truth with Dasein's disclosedness and indicates that all philosophical and everyday understandings of truth need to be connected to this more basic experience of truth. After leaving Marburg to take the position in Freiburg, Heidegger returns to these insights about truth. "On the Essence of Truth" was published in 1943, but was first delivered as a public lecture in 1930. It is tightly written and makes use of concepts that may, at least at first, seem very confusing. It is difficult to imagine an audience listening to this as a lecture and really following Heidegger. Yet, Heidegger is concerned that the path of the thought be followed.

Heidegger begins the discussion of truth much as he began *Being and Time*. First, he draws the listener or the reader's attention to the question that guides or gives rise to the process of thought that will follow. The question that is raised is not about a particular kind of truth, but about the essence of truth. He says, "The question of essence...attends to the one thing that in general distinguishes every 'truth' as truth" (BW 117). Having drawn attention to the question at issue, he also notes that the human tendency is to focus on the useful and so not ask questions such as this question about the essence of truth. When we do ask such questions, we demand an immediate answer. We are impatient and do not want to take the time to follow where the question leads. Finally, he suggests that in raising the question, we must already have some vague knowledge of truth even if we are indifferent to that knowledge. He suggests that this vague knowing combined with indifference may leave us "more desolate" than if we were completely ignorant. His remark carries the implication that this vague knowledge is also a vague knowledge of our own inauthenticity. Heidegger's reflections on truth clearly begin in the context that is established in *Being and Time*.

Our Ordinary Understanding of Truth

Heidegger begins the main part of "On the Essence of Truth" by asking what we ordinarily understand by the word "truth." This seems like a very straightforward beginning. He uses simple examples. We say that something is a true joy. The coin is true gold. In each case, we presuppose a proper meaning of joy or of gold. What we experience, the joy or the gold, is in accord with that meaning. We especially call statements true or false. If I say, "It is raining outside," the measure of the truth of that statement is whether or not it is in accord with the current weather outside my window.

In keeping with the insight in *Being and Time* that our tradition shapes us in ways that are often concealed and unrecognized, Heidegger moves to the traditional definition of truth in the medieval period. In Latin, this definition is expressed: *veritas est adequatio rei et intellectūs* (truth is the correspondence of thing and intellect). There is an ambiguity in this claim. It can indicate that truth is the correspondence of a subject matter to knowledge or of knowledge to a subject matter. Heidegger notes that Christian theology holds the two meanings together. It begins with the theological presupposition of creation and so with an interpretation of Being as God. The thing is created in accordance with an idea in the mind of God. It *is* true because it corresponds to this idea. Humans come to know the truth by conforming their minds, and so their statements, to the truth of the things. This understanding of truth presupposes God and also presupposes that human reason is a divine creation.

Heidegger points out that the understanding of truth can be

38

detached from these theological presuppositions. We recognize a rational or logical order to the world. It seems quite evident, even without presupposing divine creation, that truth is the correctness of statements. Truth is best understood as propositional truth. Heidegger says this is an old tradition of truth, "truth is the accordance (*homoiōsis*) of a statement (*logos*) with a matter (*pragma*)" (BW 122).

Heidegger moves on from this claim as if it no longer contained theological presuppositions. Yet, for the careful reader, Heidegger's statement shows that he is indirectly pointing out that the theological past and its assumptions about Being are still very much a part of our ordinary understanding of truth. The Greek words that he inserts are full of theological importance, especially for discussions of the Incarnation and how Jesus can be understood as both human and divine.

Accordance

Heidegger accepts this definition of truth that emphasizes the accordance of a statement with the subject matter. While it might be more usual to say that truth is the correspondence of the statement to the thing or to the fact, Heidegger's selection of the words that express the ordinary definition help further the rest of his analysis. He asks what we mean by accordance.

He begins with the example of two coins. If two quarters are lying on a table, we say they are "in accordance w'th one another," that is, they are the same. What we mean is that they look the same. In addition, when we say, "The quarter is round" we claim that there is an accordance, a sameness, between the quarter and the statement made about the quarter. Heidegger asks how it is that a statement and a coin are the same. They do not look alike.

Heidegger suggests that we are referring to a relationship between the coin and the statement when we say they are the same. The statement presents the coin. But the statement can only present the thing if the thing is, at least from a perspective, as the statement presents it. Heidegger says, "What is stated by the presentative statement is said of the presented thing in just such a manner *as* that thing, as presented, is" (BW 123). What Heidegger is pointing out is that the statement presents the coin as an object, distinct from or in opposition to the human subject. The statement presents the coin as the coin is related to the human speaker. The coin can be understood only in the context of the human relationship. Heidegger says that we stand open to things. We comport ourselves in relationship to them. We can speak correctly about things only from what Heidegger terms the openness of comportment.

Our relationship with other people may make this clearer. When we first meet a person, we may judge that person to be rather cold. Later, we may come to recognize the person as very warm and caring. The person has not changed, but our relationship with the person, our comportment, has changed. We say that our changed relationship enables us to know the person in a truer manner. We may even say that our original statement about the coldness of the person is not true.

Heidegger shows us that the truth of statements relies on something else, on the openness of the speaker. He concludes from this that,

> *If the correctness (truth) of statements becomes possible only through this openness of comportment, then what first makes correctness possible must with more original right be taken as the essence of truth.* (BW 124-25)

This leads to two conclusions about truth. While statements can be true or false, the essence of truth does not reside in propositions. Moreover, we need to follow this insight with an exploration of what it is that makes it possible for humans to comport themselves openly. This will provide a better grasp of the essence of truth. Heidegger continues the essay with this exploration.

Freedom

Heidegger maintains that we can be open to presenting things truthfully in statements only because we are free. We are able to accept what we encounter and let it be itself. Certainly this is the case in the example of getting to know a person. When we choose to be open towards the other person, that person can reveal him or herself to us in a richer, truer manner. Looking at the emphasis on objective truth can make the same point. When we say that we are trying to be objective, we mean that we are trying not to impose ourselves on the matter that we want to understand. We indicate that we are choosing to try to stand back and let the thing show itself to us. In each case, we can be open because we are free. Heidegger moves from this insight to the claim that the essence of truth is freedom.

Heidegger notes that it is possible to object to this claim by saying that it is too simple or too strange or by resisting the statement altogether. It may seem too simple because clearly we must be free to carry out any act, including making statements. Heidegger says that the claim that the essence of truth is freedom does not mean that truth is tied to unconstrained human action. Yet, the claim may seem strange because it suggests that truth is based on human caprice. It seems to make truth relative. What is true seems to be totally dependent on the whim of the individual subject. However, we know that humans can engage in deceit and all kinds of untruth. Finally, we may resist this claim altogether because we presuppose that truth is a property of humans. Heidegger maintains that we must uproot these presuppositions in order to think through the essence of truth as freedom. He says we must transform our thinking.

Heidegger emphasizes the need to begin this thinking from the position of finite human existence. In *Being and Time*, he emphasizes the importance of correctly formulating the questions that we pursue. He suggests that understanding is circular. We always already have a vague understanding in order to articulate an interpretation. He also emphasizes that this circular structure is not vicious. We do not simply go round and round without change. He says that it is a hermeneutical circle, a circle of understanding that can grow. Human understanding can become more open. In *Being and Time* Heidegger emphasizes the need to enter this circle in the right way. His claim that we must transform our thinking in order to think through the essence of truth as freedom is a similar claim. If we experience ourselves as Dasein, then this "experience transposes us in advance into the originally essential domain of truth" (BW 127). Heidegger suggests that to follow the way that his thinking takes requires something like a conversion experience. We must accept ourselves as disclosive, finite beings.

From the context of this experience of Dasein, freedom is best understood as open comportment. Heidegger says, "That which is opened up, that to which a presentative statement as correct corresponds, are beings opened up in an open comportment" (BW 127). Freedom is not doing what we please, or forcing ourselves on the things in the world. Freedom is letting beings be.

In explaining this phrase, to let beings be, Heidegger emphasizes that it does not mean that we neglect things. To let things be is fundamentally an engagement with things. It requires us to allow ourselves to encounter things in what Heidegger terms the open region or openness. He says that in the Western tradition this openness was first articulated in Greek with the concept *alētheia*. This word is correctly translated "truth." However, Heidegger renders the meaning more literally. It is "unconcealment." He maintains that if we begin with this understanding of truth, it is clear that freedom, as letting be, is exposing.

The English word "exposure" helps us grasp a bit more clearly what Heidegger is trying to get us to understand about truth and freedom. We can open ourselves, that is, expose ourselves to things and others in the world. This means that we place ourselves in a position such that we can be touched by other things. The example of disease is helpful here. If we expose ourselves to a disease, we go where we know that there is an outbreak of the disease. We can also be exposed to the disease. Even without knowing it, we are open to the disease and so affected by it. In language reminiscent of *Being and Time*, Heidegger says that letting be is ek-sistent. Our freedom is this relationship to entities such that they can touch us. We are engaged in "the disclosure of beings" (BW 128). We ask the question, "What are beings?" In asking this question, we experience unconcealment, that is, truth.

Heidegger also emphasizes that freedom is not a property that humans have. He says that it is more appropriate to think of freedom possessing us. Freedom makes it possible for us to have this distinctive relationship with other entities in the world. He explains human freedom as both being offered a choice and having something imposed. This is very much like Martin Luther's exposition of Christian freedom where he claims that freedom is the paradoxical situation of being subject to none, yet servant to all.

As usual, Heidegger sees the complexity of the path that he follows. If the essence of truth is freedom, and if freedom is this letting be, it is possible for humans to "also *not* let beings be the beings which they are and as they are" (BW 130). This is evident in the human ability to make untrue statements. Untruth must derive from the essence of truth.

Untruth

Heidegger recognizes that the claims that he makes seem paradoxical. He suggests that the essence of truth and untruth are the same. He follows this direction by examining untruth as concealing and as errancy.

Heidegger says that when we are engaged in letting things be, we always focus on particular entities. We comport ourselves towards those entities. In doing this, we ignore other entities, and more importantly, we conceal beings as a whole. Heidegger says that we forget the mystery of Being. We no longer ask why there is something instead of nothing. Rather, we are absorbed in asking about specific entities that we encounter. Heidegger says, "Dasein is insistent" (BW 135). We are so turned toward our own concerns that we forget the bigger picture. The language that Heidegger developed in *Being and Time* is helpful here. We are caught up in the everyday, the ontic, and so forget to think about the ontological.

Heidegger describes this situation as erring. He does not mean that we fall into occasional mistakes. Our situation is such that we are always astray. We find ourselves moving from one thing to another, wandering to-and-fro. We are dominated by this wandering and so led astray. We are in what Heidegger calls a needful condition. We are in need of questioning. Heidegger writes, "This questioning thinks the question of the *Being* of beings, a question that is essentially misleading and thus in its manifold meaning is still not mastered" (BW 137).

From Truth to Philosophy

The closing section of Heidegger's essay turns to philosophy. This may seem strange, since the essay is supposed to be about the essence of truth. Heidegger presents a very brief summary of how it is that Western philosophy has been the thinking of Being. He says that philosophical thinking is a way of questioning that does not cling solely to beings. He calls philosophy "gentle releasement." Truth is bound up with philosophical thought. Yet, because philosophy is a human activity, it too participates in the essence of truth and so also conceals. Recognizing this places contemporary philosophy in a challenging and exciting position. Philosophy is challenged to move beyond the ordinary understanding of truth. It needs to question the tradition of philosophy and develop a way of thinking that can focus on thinking as disclosing Being.

In this essay, Heidegger challenges philosophy to take seriously the task that, in much of the history of Western philosophy, has been called metaphysics. Metaphysical thought raises questions about ultimate reality, about Being. Heidegger is concerned that modern philosophy is dominated by epistemological questions, by questions that begin with knowledge as the most important philosophical questions. This approach to philosophy often overlooks and even rejects metaphysical questions. Yet, Heidegger does not think that contemporary philosophy can return to the metaphysics of the past. He judges that earlier metaphysics, like earlier theology, began with a presupposition about the nature of reality, about the nature of God. These presuppositions went unexamined. Philosophers did not ask if the concepts used in metaphysical thought were compatible with human experience. Metaphysics must not be abandoned by philosophy. But both metaphysics and philosophy in general must change. In an essay on metaphysics, written the year before the essay on truth, Heidegger writes,

> *Philosophy – what we call philosophy – is metaphysics getting under way, in which philosophy comes to itself and to its explicit tasks. Philosophy gets under way only by a peculiar insertion of our own existence into the fundamental possibilities of Dasein as a whole.* (BW 112)

The task of philosophy is to think in this manner. For Heidegger, reflections on the essence of truth confirm the importance of this philosophical work.

Heidegger sets a tremendous challenge to philosophy in this essay. It is difficult to understand how Heidegger could have, only a few years after the writing of this essay, embraced Nazism. Did he forget what he had recognized about human existence and its tendency to get caught up in the everyday? Was he convinced that he could become the philosophical voice of National Socialism and so call people to an awareness of who they were? Did he become so evangelical about his own philosophical position that he forgot that philosophy too is always erring? Many contemporary thinkers have pondered these questions and searched Heidegger's work for answers, and there are many different responses to these questions. As noted in the first chapter, Heidegger does not speak to these questions and so they do not become guiding questions for his thought.

Heidegger does not abandon his thinking on truth. He has proposed that philosophy must think this question and many other questions in a new way once the finite human situation is appropriately experienced. In 1935, Heidegger turns to art.

44

5
Art

After resigning from the position of Rector at the University of Freiburg, Heidegger returned to lecturing. In 1935 and 1936, he presented several public lectures in Freiburg, Zürich, and Frankfurt. A finalized version of these lectures, "The Origin of the Work of Art," was not published until 1950. However, Hans-Georg Gadamer reports that these lectures had tremendous philosophical influence before the publication of the essay. Indeed, they caused a philosophical sensation (Gadamer 98-99). In *Being and Time*, Heidegger had already developed a concept of 'world.' World is not understood as the totality of things that are present-at-hand. Rather, Heidegger's concept of world is based on the New Testament concept of world that is anthropological. World is that whole in which Dasein develops self-understanding, self-interpretation. Those familiar with Heidegger's work were not surprised by his continued use of this concept of world. However, Heidegger introduced a new concept, 'earth,' and this was part of the cause of the sensation.

The introduction of the concept of earth is sometimes taken as Heidegger's turn to mythology. He had been reading and lecturing on Hölderlin during this period, and probably gets the term from Hölderlin's poetry. Yet, in focusing on the work of art and in introducing this new concept, Heidegger is moving along the path that he set out on in "On the Essence of Truth." In that essay he described the tension between truth as unconcealment and the concealment that also seems to be part of the essence of truth. In "The Origin of the

Work of Art," Heidegger turns to art because it is an especially appropriate example of the event of truth. It is a place to begin thinking the implications of the tension of truth more fully.

In his usual manner, Heidegger begins by posing a question for thinking to try to follow. His question is about the origin of the work of art. Clearly, we can say that a work of art has its origin in an artist. But Heidegger notes that it is just as accurate to say that the artist is an artist because of the work of art. "The artist is the origin of the work. The work is the origin of the artist" (BW 149).

Heidegger reiterates the circular character of thinking that he described in *Being and Time*. He writes,

> *Thus we are compelled to follow the circle. This is neither a makeshift nor a defect. To enter upon this path is the strength of thought, to continue on it is the feast of thought, assuming that thinking is a craft. Not only is the main step from the work to art a circle like the step from art to work, but every separate step that we attempt circles in this circle.* (BW 150)

It is important to try to follow Heidegger's circling path rather than to simply summarize his philosophical concepts.

To begin, Heidegger notes that works of art are most simply things. They are present in our world. The picture hangs on the office wall beside the calendar and the to-do list. The book of poetry sits on the shelf. All of these things can be packed in boxes and moved to another office or stored away. The tendency is to acknowledge that art has the character of a thing, and then to ask what distinguishes art as a work from other sorts of things. In his usual manner, Heidegger asks us to pause and consider whether this is the best approach. He asks that we take time to examine where we are before proceeding. He asks, "What in truth is the thing, so far as it is a thing?"

Thing and Work

Heidegger notes that in common usage the word "thing" refers to everything including God and death. But we also narrow the term to refer to "mere things." We use the term in this manner to refer to "lifeless beings of nature and objects of use" (BW 152). We refer to stones and pencils as things. In addition to common usage, we can call on philosophy to begin a search for the character of the thing.

Philosophical Interpretations

Philosophy in the Western tradition has developed three basic interpretations of the thing. A thing is a bearer of traits or properties, a manifold of what is given in the senses, or matter, which is formed.

Heidegger looks first at the interpretation of the thing that says it is a substance that bears properties. A thing has properties. For example, this book has pages. Heidegger dismisses this concept for a number of reasons. He finds it suspicious that the concept so closely reflects the structure of sentences. It appears that this concept imposes an interpretation and so may actually serve to conceal the nature of a thing. Heidegger says it keeps things at a distance from us. The second interpretation of a thing suggests that it is what can be perceived by the senses. A thing can be heard, smelled, seen, tasted, and touched. We hear the water running from the fountain, smell its odor, see it sparkle in the sun, taste its coolness, and touch its wetness. The thing is the unity of all that is given in the senses. Heidegger suggests that this interpretation seems as convincing as the first interpretation. However, it is also a problematic interpretation. Heidegger says, we never first perceive a group of sensations. Rather, we experience the water. We need an interpretation that will allow the thing "to remain in its self-containment" (BW 157).

The third interpretation is helpful in this regard. This interpretation holds that a thing is formed matter. It is a synthesis of matter and form. Thus, we can understand the way in which a work of art is a thing. Matter is formed by the artist's action. Heidegger anticipates the reader's question. Why bother rejecting the first two interpretations? Why not just proceed to the preferred interpretation? He says that he did not begin with this interpretation because he also mistrusts it. He shows how this particular interpretation is modeled on the action of a craftsperson and on the useful or equipment value of things. The craftsperson makes things that are useful, that have a function. Even God, in the act of creating things is understood as acting within this model. Again, Heidegger says that our interpretation forces itself on things.

A Clue

The purpose of the essay up to this point is to demonstrate the preconceptions that we need to be aware of as we carry out the rest of the analysis. However, Heidegger suggests that it has given us a clue. The third interpretation has been the most dominant interpretation in the Western tradition. This may well be the case because equipment is the result of human making and so is familiar to us. Equipment is more than a mere thing, but not yet a work of art. Heidegger suggests that an examination of the equipment may help distinguish thing, equipment, and work. The task will be to avoid making equipment primary and thing and work derivative from equipment. In order to do this, he selects an example of equipment, a pair of shoes. But he chooses to describe the shoes from Van Gogh's paintings of a peasant's shoes.

He carries out a description of the painting, showing that the shoes reveal the whole world of life of a rural peasant woman. The worn shoes reveal the labor and the joy of the woman's life. They reveal her anxiety and show how she belongs to the earth. This is his first introduction of the term "earth" which will become important for the development of the essay. Moreover, Heidegger claims that it is reliability that makes the shoes what they are. Because the shoes are reliable, the woman can carry out her work in the world. Heidegger says that reliability is the being, or essence, of equipment. Something has the nature of equipment, not because it is made by humans and not because it is useful. Equipment is reliable. The reliability of the shoes enables the woman to be secure in the world and to belong to the earth.

This description may appear overly romantic, especially to someone who has worked a farm. However, Heidegger is at least in part developing the description to draw us in. He pauses and suggests that we have lost our way. We started out to ask about the work of art. What we have learned is something about equipment. But wait; "unwittingly" we have learned something about the work of art (BW 164).

The Event of Truth

Heidegger says that the painting spoke. We often use this expression of art. We say that music, poetry, and painting speak to us. Heidegger maintains that what art does is show us the truth of things.

48

Van Gogh's painting has shown what the shoes, in truth, are. At the same time, we have learned about the work of art. Heidegger writes, "By this means, almost clandestinely, it came to light what is at work in the work: The disclosure of the particular being in its being, the happening of truth" (BW 165). Art is an event of truth; it is "truth setting itself to work" (BW 166).

Heidegger's approach is contrived, but the conclusion that he draws from his analysis must be part of why this essay, when first delivered as lectures, was recognized as philosophically so important. The most immediate reality of the work of art is not that it is a thing, but that it is an event of truth. The second part of Heidegger's essay develops this claim.

The Work and Truth

The second part of "The Origin of the Work of Art" meditates on the claim that art is truth setting itself to work. Heidegger maintains that art that has been removed from the space, either physical or temporal, where it belongs is just an object. It no longer performs the work that is appropriate for a work of art. In order to focus on the work of truth that happens in a work of art, Heidegger elects to describe a non-representational work of art that is in the physical and social context where it belongs. He reflects on a Greek temple, not as an artifact of history, but in the time when it served as a temple for a god. The temple stands on rocky ground and encloses the figure of a god. It shelters the god from the thunderstorms and heat. Heidegger uses the temple to exemplify that as a work, the temple does two things. It sets up a world and sets forth the earth.

It is important to make use of the language that Heidegger uses as he develops his philosophy. He avoids concepts that carry presuppositions about the nature of truth and of human existence. He tries to develop language that will express more fully the philosophical insights that he follows. In following Heidegger, the reader can fall into either of two pitfalls. We can embrace the language and be "Heidegerrized" without really following Heidegger's thinking. We can also try to explain Heidegger with more usual philosophical language and also fail to grasp his thinking. It is particularly difficult at this point to follow Heidegger without falling into one or the other of these dangers as we try to understand what he means by "world" and "earth."

49

World

In *Being and Time* Heidegger developed the concept of world. In "The Origin of the Work of Art," he is calling on that concept. But he is hesitant to begin with a mere repetition of what he has already developed. Rather, he says that for the path he is on, it is better to try to prevent distortion of the world. He does not want us to understand world as a concept. He says that the world is not an object. It is not a framework that we bring to what is given. The most positive direction that he gives for understanding world is when he says "the world worlds" (BW 170). It is no wonder that his thought can be frustrating. Yet, in describing world in this manner, Heidegger emphasizes that the world is not static, nor is it separate from us. We need to find a way to speak about the world as opening through which things become near and far, are lingering and hastening. We need to find a way that enables us to experience world.

Heidegger's approach here is similar to that taken in *Being and Time*. He is concerned that his thinking do more than provide philosophical concepts. He tries to lead us to a new experience of Dasein, of our human finitude. At the end of *Being and Time*, Heidegger arrives at the recognition of the historicality of Dasein. We are shaped by the communities and traditions in which we find ourselves. This insight is of growing importance to Heidegger as he reflects on art and truth.

The process of setting up a world is not individual. Heidegger says, "the world is the self-opening openness of the broad paths of the simple and essential decisions in the destiny of an historical people" (BW 172). The temple as work sets up a world through its consecration and dedication. The temple sets up a world in such a way as to invoke the presence of the god. It opens the space "out of which the protective grace of the gods is granted or withheld" (BW 170-171). The world is a realm of unconcealedness. It is what Heidegger terms the Open.

Earth

Heidegger says, the work not only sets up a world, it also sets forth the earth. The easiest way to begin to understand Heidegger's point is to recognize that every work of art makes use of material. The temple is made of stone. When the stone is used to make the temple, a world is set up. The stone is also brought into the openness of the world. However, the stone remains undisclosed in the world that it helps set up. Heidegger emphasizes that the materials used in creating a work do not end up as what is revealed or understood in the work. The temple certainly is made of stone. But it is not about stone. It is about religious experience and the human relationship to the divine. Heidegger says, there is no trace of the work material in the work. When people worship at the temple, they do not say "what beautiful stone." Rather, they experience the presence, or even the absence, of the god. Heidegger says, "The earth is the spontaneous forthcoming of that which is continually self-secluding and to that extent sheltering and concealing" (BW 172).

Relation of World and Earth

World and earth are not separate, but are interconnected. The world rests on the earth and tries to overcome the inherent concealedness of the earth. The earth pulls the world in and tries to keep it there. Like a flowering plant, the world is embedded in the earth and yet rises above it and opens its flowers. The tension and striving that Heidegger describes here are similar to the tension between the everyday inauthentic tendency to gossip and cover over, and the authentic desire of Dasein to know itself in its totality. In *Being and Time* Heidegger emphasizes that we cannot escape the everyday. But, he retains a sense that the authentic can rise above the inauthentic, if only briefly. The transition from the concept of the "everyday" to the concept "earth" emphasizes what Heidegger develops in "On the Essence of Truth." Concealedness belongs to truth as unconcealedness. Heidegger writes,

> *The world is the clearing of the paths of the essential guiding directions with which all decision complies. Every decision, however, bases itself on something not mastered, something concealed, confusing; else it would never be a decision.* (BW 177)

The task is not to separate ourselves from our earthly existence. The task is to recognize the tension for what it is. Truth happens when this tension or play between clearing and concealing becomes evident to us. This tension or play becomes evident only when it enters into history.

51

One of the ways this happens is in the work of art. Heidegger's path has taken him from an experience of a work of art to the question: What is truth, that it can happen, and perhaps must happen, as art?

Truth and Art

The third section of "The Origin of the Work of Art" addresses the question as to why truth happens as art by looking at art as creation, as preservation, and at poetry as the paradigm for art. Heidegger begins by noting that he has not looked at art as the creation of the artist in the first two sections of the essay. He does not emphasize the genius of the artist. This is not because Heidegger thinks that artists are untalented or unimportant. However, Heidegger continues to emphasize the importance of the human community and tradition and the way in which truth happens in the community. He says that truth can happen in a variety of ways. While the work of art is a primary and privileged event of truth, the foundation of political state, the essential sacrifice (perhaps the crucifixion), and the thinker's questioning are also ways in which truth happens. All of these are sources of people's historical existence. Truth always comes into existence historically. Heidegger develops this by looking at creation, preservation, and poetry.

Creating

Heidegger maintains that creation, which all art is, is fundamentally a knowing, not a making. He recognizes that there is a tendency to view both art and crafts as a type of making. Art simply has some additional quality added to the making. It is more creative. As is his way, he questions this approach to creation.

He notes that the Greeks used the word *technē* for both art and crafts. This was not because art was a type of craft. Rather both art and crafts were understood as modes of knowing. They are both ways of apprehending what is present. The craftsperson apprehends things as equipment. For example, the potter understands the clay and can make bowls and plates out of the clay. The craftsperson uses up the clay in making the dishes ready for use. The artist also understands the clay. But what the artist brings forth is a creation.

Heidegger emphasizes two characteristics of createdness. He says

52

that createdness always reveals the conflict between "lighting and concealing in the opposition of world and earth" (BW 181). He calls this opposition or conflict the rift (*Riss*). A work of art is a creation because it shows us the conflictual nature of historical human existence. It also shows us that we cannot escape this tension. The two poles cannot be separated. We can never have total clarity or unconcealedness. Truth is never purely present. It is always present in a finite historical context. It is always mixed with concealment or untruth. The work of art holds this tension before us so that we can recognize it as our human situation. Heidegger says that the work of art fixes the truth.

While Heidegger does not mention them, Michelangelo's "Captives," figures that he sculpted in their incompleteness coming out of the stone exemplify Heidegger's point. These figures reach towards a world of openness, but at the same time are not free from the stone. They show us the tension of our historical existence.

The work of art not only shows us this rift. It also shows us that the work is created. This does not mean that it primarily reveals the hand of a great artist, a genius. It does need a creator, but the creator is not what is presented in the work. The work of art announces that unconcealedness has happened and that is has happened in the work. While this may seem complicated, in some ways this is a simple insight. The sculptures of Michelangelo show us not only the tension of human existence, they also show us that we are being shown that tension.

Preserving

Heidegger says that when we recognize that the work of art is an event of truth and try to stay within the truth that happens there, we preserve the work of art. He writes, "Just as a work cannot be without being created but is essentially in need of creators, so what is created cannot itself come into being without those who preserve it." He emphasizes that this does not mean that we preserve art in our private experiences or feelings of the art. To preserve the work of art is to participate in the truth that happens in the work. Both creating and preserving are part of art. Heidegger writes, "art is the creative preserving of truth in the work. *Art then is the becoming and happening of truth*" (BW 183). To preserve the work of art is not to hang it in a museum or to keep it from falling down. To preserve the work is to perpetuate the truth that is set forth in the work. It is to hand it over as a living work within the context of human history.

Poetry

At the end of "The Origin of the Work of Art," Heidegger makes a leap to the art of poetry. He says, "Truth, as the lighting and concealing of beings, happens in being composed. *All art*, as the letting happen of the advent of the truth of beings, is as such, *in essence, poetry*" (BW 184). While Heidegger suggests that language is essentially poetry, he also privileges poetry as the work of art that most clearly shows us the nature of art as the event of truth. Poetry shows us that both creating and preserving are essential to the work of art, and to truth. Poetry transports a people. It gives them a sense of themselves and challenges them to be true to what is presented in the poetry. Heidegger suggests that Hölderlin's poetry especially confronts the German people with their historical situation.

Reflecting on Heidegger's Path

"The Origin of the Work of Art" moves Heidegger in the direction of language. He certainly recognized the importance of language for Dasein's structure of understanding in *Being and Time*. But the reflections on truth and art as well as his reading of Hölderlin lead Heidegger to recognize that language is the place or the medium in which truth takes place. We live in language. If we are to understand our finitude with all of its historical implications, we must ask questions about the nature of language.

Before turning to Heidegger's work on language, however, it is worth taking a bit of a detour to consider his reflections on humanism.

6

Humanism

Shortly after the end of World War II, Jean-Paul Sartre delivered a public address, *Existentialism Is a Humanism*. Reports claim that the city of Paris was quiet because everyone was at the lecture. Whether or not those reports are true, the lecture had considerable impact. Jean Beaufret wanted to distinguish Sartre's form of existentialism from Heidegger's thought and to engage the two great thinkers in conversation. On November 10, 1946, Beaufret wrote Heidegger three questions. He asked Heidegger to reflect on how it might be possible to restore meaning to the word "humanism." He sought Heidegger's thought on the relation of his philosophy to an ethics. He asked how it might be possible to preserve a sense of adventure in philosophy without making that the only point of philosophy. Heidegger had been in isolation since the end of the war, unable to teach. He probably appreciated the opportunity to again engage others in philosophical thought. In response to Beaufret, Heidegger wrote his "Letter on Humanism."

This work is one of Heidegger's most readable essays. He makes use of the analysis of Dasein in *Being and Time* and explains his thinking as it emerges after this book. This is a particularly helpful essay for understanding Heidegger's thought and the sort of transformation that he thinks is necessary for both finite humans and for philosophy.

The Question of Humanism

Heidegger focuses on Beaufret's question: "How can we restore meaning to the word 'humanism'?" He realizes that Beaufret's concerns arise from reading Heidegger's work, especially *Being and Time*, in the light of Sartre's thought and in the light of the inhumanity exposed in World War II. The question that is being raised is really how the human situation can be understood in the face of the holocaust. Heidegger never says this directly. However, it is the unspoken background for the conversation that Beaufret initiates. Sartre has responded to the situation by rejecting God and Christian humanism as well as communism. The existentialism that Sartre develops places primary emphasis on human choice and action. In doing this, he stresses the fundamental importance of the human subject.

Heidegger begins his letter without mentioning Sartre. However, the context that he sets for addressing Beaufret's questions emphasizes his differences with Sartre. He remarks that action is best understood as accomplishment. He holds that thinking is what humans accomplish. Thinking is not a making or a causing. Rather, "in thinking Being comes to language." Heidegger expands on this position claiming that humans dwell in the house of Being. He writes,

> *Language is the house of Being.... Those who think and those who create with words are the guardians of this home. Their guardianship accomplishes the manifestation of Being insofar as they bring the manifestation to language and maintain it in language through their speech.* (BW 193)

While the letter does address Beaufret's questions, it does so out of the context of, and in an attempt to explain, this claim.

Thinking and Technē

Heidegger suggests that it may not be necessary to retain the word "humanism." He suggests this because he maintains that it is very easy for thinking to slip into what he calls technē. A technē is an instrument that serves what Heidegger called the "they" in *Being and Time*. It is a technique, an instrument of education. When thinking becomes a technique, Heidegger says that it falls under the dictatorship of the public realm. The public realm takes subjectivity to be fundamental. Everything is understood in terms of the everyday needs and desires of humans. The public realm defines those needs and sets the parameters for how the needs will be met. Heidegger says that every –ism is such an articulating of human desire. This public realm cannot be escaped by fleeing to the private as the location of freedom. Simply negating that which the public defines for human desire is not a way of regaining authentic thinking. The language of thinking is in the service of communication that dominates and controls.

If humans are to think purely or authentically, thinking must be freed from technē. It must be freed from a technical interpretation that places reflection in the service of doing and making. Heidegger maintains that the path to freeing thinking requires reflection on the essence of langu ̣e. This reflection cannot begin with presupposed concepts. He says that we "must first learn to exist in the nameless" (BW 199). Heidegger emphasizes that the thinking that he is trying to facilitate calls for us to be claimed by Being. We must listen before we speak and try to articulate this claim that is made on us.

Heidegger says that insofar as his thinking emphasizes the importance of being claimed, there is a concern about the human. His position is humanism in that it meditates on what it is to be human and it cares that we not be inhumane. He wants us to understand what it is to be a finite human and to live within the fullness of that possibility. He is concerned about human essence, about what it is to be human.

Humanism and Metaphysics

Even though his thinking is concerned with the human, Heidegger is hesitant to use the word "humanism" to apply to this thought. In part, this is because humanism refers to positions that hold to a number of very different understandings of what it means to be human. He notes that all forms of humanism are concerned that humans be free for and find worth in their humanity. Yet, each understands freedom and human nature differently.

To illustrate his point, he reviews the dominant forms of humanism: Christian humanism, Marxism, and Enlightenment humanism with its roots in the Roman Republic. All of these types of humanism, and Sartre's existentialism as yet another form of humanism, differ in their basic understandings. Marxism views humans as essentially social, meeting their natural needs together. Christianity views humans as essentially children of God, essentially not of this world. Heidegger concludes,

> *However different these forms of humanism may be in purpose and in principle, in the mode and means of their respective realizations, and in the form of their teaching, they nonetheless all agree in this, that the <u>humanitas</u> of <u>homo humanus</u> is determined with regard to an already established interpretation of nature, history, world, and the ground of the world, that is, of beings as a whole.* (BW 201-202)

All forms of humanism have metaphysical presuppositions. Our metaphysical presuppositions are the assumptions about the nature of ultimate reality that come before and give the framework for all of our other understandings. Heidegger repeats the claim with which he began *Being and Time*. Metaphysics does not ask about the truth of Being. Because of this, "Being is still waiting for the time when it will become thought-provoking" (BW 203). Metaphysics in all forms fails to recognize that to be human is to be claimed by Being.

Ek-sistence

Heidegger maintains that openness to the recognition of the claim of Being is "standing in the lighting of Being." He calls this standing in the light, "Ek-sistence." He used this term in essays that he wrote in the 1930s, but now it takes a central role in his thought. The term is closely connected to the term "ecstasis" that Heidegger used in *Being and Time*. It indicates that humans always find themselves outside of themselves, or "standing out." In addition, in this letter Heidegger uses the term to emphasize that humans are unique in their relationship to Being.

Heidegger even makes the claim that "The human body is something essentially other than an animal organism" (BW 204). He does not mean that there is no possible scientific explanation of the human body. However, scientific explanation cannot provide an understanding of human essence. Nor can an understanding of what is essentially human be gained by simply adding a soul or mind to the scientifically explained body.

Heidegger develops his understanding of Dasein with this claim that the human essence is ek-sistence. He says that the "Da," the there, is the lighting of Being. To be human is to stand outside of ourselves in the truth of Being. To be human is to inherit the truth of Being. Heidegger does not claim that we will find this way of thinking about ourselves easy. It would be much easier to be a humanist of one form or another. Yet, he claims that if we can transform our thought to think our nature as ek-sistence, we will be able to realize a more proper human dignity. He says that we will come to understand that to be human is to be the shepherd of Being. What is essential is Being.

Being

Heidegger uses the term "Being" extensively. In the process, he often sketches what he does not mean. Being should not be understood as God or as some cosmic ground. He rarely gives a direct explanation of what he does mean. This is, of course, because he is trying to help us break out of or overcome traditional metaphysics. Yet, he retains the word "Being." This can be frustrating for the reader. We want an answer from Heidegger. What is Being?

In the "Letter on Humanism" he offers a hint toward an answer. "It is It itself." Heidegger asks us not to be impatient with this response. He says, "The thinking that is to come must learn to experience that and to say it" (BW 210).

In order to learn to experience this, Heidegger suggests that we must turn to what is nearest. He says that Being is so near that it seems far. It is so close that we miss it. He says that Being is something simple. "As such, Being remains mysterious, the simple nearness of an unobtrusive governance. The nearness occurs essentially as language itself" (BW 212). If we are to be the shepherds of Being, we must live in language. We must think by trying to find the right words for the human relationship to Being.

Thinking

Heidegger's hints about Being are simple and minimal. However, his letter devotes considerable reflection to what he means by "thinking." In the course of these reflections he describes the historical relationship of thinking to metaphysics. He also develops an explanation of the experience of homelessness as part of the impetus for thinking. Finally, he reflects on the relationship of thinking to logic, God, and ethics.

Historicity

Heidegger maintains that thinking must direct itself towards saying Being in its truth. Yet, thinking is historical. Heidegger emphasizes the importance of what he called the historicity of Dasein in *Being and Time*. We are historical, not because things happen to us over the course of time. We are historical because we already are that which has been. We are formed by our traditions and communities. We receive our being in that process. Thinking must always remember that it is historical.

This means that thinking cannot declare all past thinking about Being to be false. Thinking must not ignore previous philosophy. Even if this philosophy has become ensnared in metaphysical thought that serves to conceal Being, we cannot start fresh as if this thought had never happened. Our thinking stands within the tradition of this thought. What thinking must do is to find ways to question metaphysics so that Being can be revealed. Many of Heidegger's lecture courses focused on this task. He believes that in order to move into thinking, we must struggle with the thinkers who have shaped our thought. Heidegger often claims that his task is to overcome metaphysics. Yet, he does not want to annihilate metaphysics. He want to think through metaphysical thought in order to achieve thinking.

Our historical nature not only means that metaphysics remains important, it also means that we do not produce Being. Being is something that we receive. Heidegger plays with the German expression "Es gibt." This means "there is" but it also can be translated "it gives." We experience our ek-sistence as given.

Homelessness

Thinking must develop in relationship to metaphysical thought as it is given to us. Yet, metaphysical thought leads to an experience that moves us towards thinking. Heidegger calls this the experience of homelessness. He says the Friedrich Nietzsche was the last philosopher to experience homelessness. This makes Nietzsche's thought particularly important for us. What Nietzsche experienced was that there is no way out of metaphysics. This experience can be called the death of God. It can be called nihilism. But it is the experience of the inability of metaphysical thought to show us who we are. Heidegger says that this is because metaphysics has focused on our ability to master beings. This is not who we are.

Once we have experienced our homelessness, however, we are able to be called home. For Heidegger, it is in the voice of the poetry of Hölderlin that he hears this calling. In the "Letter on Humanism," Heidegger emphasizes that this calling home should not be understood as a call to nationalism. Clearly, Heidegger does not want to be misunderstood as advocating a political position. To be called home is to recognize that we are not the lord of beings, but the shepherd of Being, the "neighbor of Being" (BW 222). Philosophy must not protect itself from or resist the shock of this experience. This means that philosophy must maintain a proper silence. It also means that we will not know if we are following a blind alley until we have tried the way. Heidegger explains a bit more fully what he means by offering some reflections on the relationship of thinking to logic, to claims about God, and to ethics.

Thinking and Resistance

Heidegger reflects on the possibility of keeping the word "humanism" for the thinking that he advocates. While what he advocates contradicts the other positions that use this term, keeping the term would emphasize that his position is not inhumane. Yet, resisting using the term may provide the shock that thinking needs. This is the position that Heidegger chooses. He notes that his thinking in *Being and Time* has already been misinterpreted. Rather than embrace the term "humanism," it is better to continue to set out language that shocks people. This may serve to awaken the sort of reflection that Heidegger believes contemporary humanity needs.

Heidegger notes that his thought has been termed illogical, atheistic, and nihilistic. He is charged with abandoning rigorous thinking and advocating arbitrary feeling. What he really advocates is resistance, thinking against logic. This means rigorously thinking the essence of *logos*. He is charged with being indifferent in relation to questions about God. Yet, his work clearly is concerned with these questions. He says that his thought has not decided in favor of theism, "out of respect for the boundaries that have been set for thinking as such" (BW 230). If his thought has led people to think about these issues, then being misunderstood serves an important purpose. It has directed others toward thinking.

Heidegger develops the example of resisting ethics in more detail in order to make his point. Resistance of commonly accepted concepts can push us to the thinking that is needed. Ethics is normally understood as rules or principles of action. Heidegger resists this understanding by reflecting on Heraclitus, a pre-Socratic thinker. He maintains that for Heraclitus the word ēthos indicated an abode or dwelling place. Ethics thinks about human dwelling. Heidegger illustrates the significance of this understanding with a story about Heraclitus. Heraclitus is said to have had visitors come to see the great thinker, only to find him warming himself by his stove. His visitors were perplexed when he called for them to join him saying, "here too the gods are present" (BW 233). Heidegger takes this to mean that thinking about how humans dwell is more fundamental than developing an ethics.

Heidegger maintains that such thinking is neither theoretical nor practical. Thinking is prior to this distinction. He says that thinking is a deed, but not in the sense of a practical action that assigns a direction to human life, that provides us with a rule by which to live. He writes,

> *Thinking towers above action and production, not through the grandeur of its achievement and not as a consequence of its effect, but through the humbleness of its inconsequential accomplishment.* (BW 239)

Thinking is best carried out as poetry. Thinking is learning to dwell poetically, "For thinking in its saying merely brings the unspoken word of Being to language" (BW 239).

Resisting logic, theology, and ethics may shock us out of our complacency in metaphysics and help us understand what it is to dwell poetically. Heidegger suggests that resisting the use of the concept "humanism" will serve a similar purpose.

Advent

Heidegger concludes his letter by turning to Beaufret's third question about preserving the adventure of philosophy without reducing philosophy to mere adventure. Heidegger plays with the language of Beaufret's question and says, "Thinking as such is bound to the advent of Being, to Being as advent" (BW 241). Heidegger's play is helpful for understanding his point. Advent is the season in the Christian calendar that awaits the birth of Jesus. A birth is not something that can be known in advance. It requires patient and careful waiting. Birth happens to both the mother and the child. Neither chooses the time or the means of the birth. Those involved with the birth must be ready to attend to the delivery and to alter what they do in relationship to the child's arrival. Giving birth involves tremendous risk. Yet, it is so natural that it goes unnoticed.

Heidegger says similar things about thinking. He says that thinking must bind itself to the fittingness of "the saying of Being." Thinking must develop a "rigor of meditation, carefulness in saying, frugality with words" (BW 241). Such thinking must not overestimate philosophy. The thinking that is called for is no longer philosophy, at least in the sense of metaphysics. It is certainly not philosophy in the sense of twentieth-century philosophy of language and epistemology. Thinking must do its work inconspicuously in language. Heidegger makes one of his most famous claims in closing, "In this way language is the language of Being, as clouds are the clouds of the sky" (BW 242). His reflections on truth, art, and humanism all lead him to language.

7

Language

After Heidegger was reinstated to the faculty and received emeritus status at the University of Freiburg in 1950, he focused many of his lectures and essays on the topic of language. Much of twentieth-century philosophy has focused on language. A great deal of this thought is influenced by a philosophical approach that develops early in the century, logical positivism. The thought of Ludwig Wittgenstein is also important for contemporary philosophy of language. Heidegger's thought is developed in clear distinction from the sort of philosophy of language that is influenced by logical positivism. Indeed, the issue of language clearly illustrates some of the major distinctions between the two strands of twentieth-century philosophy, analytical and continental. Heidegger's thought is not influenced by the work of Wittgenstein, although comparison of the two thinkers has provided insight into ways in which the two directions of philosophical thought can complement each other.

In order to avoid the dominance of philosophical logic, Heidegger seeks insight from pre-Socratic thinkers. He turns to these thinkers in the hope of finding clues for thinking the human relationship to language in a manner that does not presuppose the influence of Aristotle's logic. The sayings of Heraclitus about *logos* are particularly important for Heidegger's thought. He retrieves Heraclitus' understanding of *logos*. In addition, Heidegger emphasizes the importance of beginning thinking about the nature of language from the position that his work has made possible. He develops and uses the

64

term *Ereignis* for this situation. While the word literally translates, "Event," Heidegger's use is inventive and important to his developing thought. A summary of Heidegger's retrieval of *logos* and of his development of *Ereignis* help introduce his thought on language.

Retrieving *Logos*

Heidegger began *Being and Time* by claiming that what philosophy must do is to retrieve the question of Being. While, over the course of twenty-five years, his thought moves from a focus on Dasein to a focus on language, he continues to emphasize the importance of retrieval. Retrieval is a philosophical process in which we look back into the history of philosophy in order to try to think a question or concept in a more original way. We recognize that our contemporary thought about the matter leads us astray. In going back to earlier thought, we try to identify aspects of that thought that were never developed. They were lost or forgotten over time. Heidegger maintains that these aspects still remain unsaid, and so provide us with possibilities for thought.

Heidegger already recognized the importance of language when he wrote *Being and Time*. He connects both the method of phenomenology and his brief comments about language to the Greek word *logos*. In his early thought, he is primarily concerned with *logos* insofar as it indicates a "making manifest" or "disclosure." In 1951, he presents a lecture in which he attempts to retrieve the concept of *logos*. The lecture is translated in *Early Greek Thinking*, and is titled simply "*Logos*." In the lecture, Heidegger makes use of the derivation of the word as he develops it out of a single fragment of Heraclitus' thought He works out the derivation in order to provide direction for contemporary thinking about language.

Derivation

Heidegger's use of etymologies for developing philosophical thought is controversial. Some thinkers find his etymologies accurate and exceedingly helpful. Others believe that he invents these etymologies to serve his own purposes. Even if the etymology that Heidegger develops for *logos* is inaccurate, it is helpful for

65

understanding the direction that his thought takes in approaching the nature of language.

Heidegger notes that the Greek word *logos* is derived from *legein* which is usually taken to mean "to speak." He argues that there is an earlier meaning for the Greek that is related to the German word *legen*, "to lay down and lay before." Heidegger then says that *legen* is closely connected with *lesen* which means "to read," but which also means "to glean or gather." From this Heidegger says that *legein* is a laying down and laying before that gathers both itself and the other.

Heidegger develops this emphasis on gathering by means of an example. He says that harvesting is a form of gathering. When the corn is harvested, it is gathered into a place for safe-keeping. It is sheltered and preserved. In addition, only the corn that is dry enough so that it will not rot is brought in. There is a selecting that occurs in the process of gathering and preserving. Those who do the selecting, the people who gather the corn, are also already gathered. That is, they have the proper clothing and equipment.

Whether Heidegger provides a derivation of *logos*, or simply invents a story in order to retrieve what he thinks is important for beginning to think about language, his main point is that we need to understand *logos* as a presenting event of gathering and sheltering. When we understand this, we also recognize that this gathering includes us.

Direction

Heidegger's derivational work on *logos*, serves to set him on a way in his thinking about language. Human speaking cannot be understood as a purely autonomous human act. Language is not a tool, invented and used by humans. It is not something handy in the world. Just as *Being and Time* provides a new view of what it is to be human, Heidegger's reflections on *logos* provide a starting point for a new view of language. Language, understood as *logos*, may be a way of experiencing Being that is more helpful than the Dasein analysis. We are gathered into language, and yet we speak. In the event of language, we may be able to experience and articulate our relationship to Being in ways that were not possible in the earlier work.

Ereignis

Before focusing on some of the themes that Heidegger develops in his considerations of language, it is important to look briefly at the concept of *Ereignis*. While Heidegger makes use of etymologies to develop his thinking, he also plays with the German language, adopting and adapting in order to attempt to articulate his interpretations. *Ereignis* is a term that becomes central for his thought.

In German, the verb *ereignen* means "to happen.' The noun, *Ereignis* means "event." The concept of an event is important to Heidegger's thought even in its earliest expressions. The choice of temporality to articulate the structure of Dasein illustrates this importance. His use of the expression "It gives" in "The Origin of the Work of Art" also points to an event structure. Language that calls on event structure appeals to him because of the movement that is implied. He constantly struggles to avoid introducing language that presupposes a static philosophical view or a metaphysics that emphasizes that reality is best understood as substance.

The word *Ereignis* is connected to *eigen*, 'one's own,' and to *eigentlich* 'authentic.' Heidegger's use of the term calls on both of these connections. The event structure that he tries to articulate is an event of appropriation. This event of appropriation shows us that we make things our own. However, Heidegger does not mean that in appropriation we dominate. The connection with authenticity helps make this clearer. In *Being and Time*, authenticity indicates the possibility for Dasein of recognizing its own nature as disclosive of Being. *Eriegnis* is an event of appropriation and disclosure.

In some of his later essays, Heidegger develops the understanding of this appropriating and disclosing event as a mirroring or a play. He introduces language about a fourfold that he terms earth, sky, divinity, and mortals. This language is reminiscent of the language of world and earth that he used in "The Origin of the Work of Art." Again what Heidegger tries to do is shock us into thinking in a new way. *Ereignis* is an appropriating and disclosing event in which each element lights up and reflects the others.

Simple examples give some illustration of what Heidegger is trying to express. A still lake reflects the sky and clouds, the mountain at its shore, and our face as we look into the water. If the clouds block the sun, or if we ripple the water, the reflection is broken, but the play continues. There is a back-and-forth movement in which the world is disclosed. A conversation is a better illustratation of the play that concerns Heidegger. In a conversation, we are absorbed in what is said. We exchange ideas. In the process, we learn about each other and we disclose ourselves to each other. If it is a productive conversation, we are changed and come to know ourselves better.

Ereignis is an event of appropriating and disclosing where we are as much appropriated as appropriators. We are gathered into a situation where we belong together with what is present with us. We disclose the world like the mirroring of the lake. We reflect things in the context of the light that is available.

The concept of *Ereignis* is extremely important for Heidegger's understanding of language. When this concept is paired with his interpretaion of *logos*, it is easier to understand his claim that language is the house of Being. This claim indicates that language is this event of appropriating and disclosing. If we think about language, we may be able to understand ourselves and our relation to Being more appropriately.

Language as Saying

Most of Heidegger's writing on language is translated into English in *On the Way to Language*, which was first published in German in 1959. In addition, "Language," one of the essays that is in the original German volume, is translated in *Poetry, Language, Thought*. Heidegger writes of his approach to language,

> *When we reflect on language qua language, we have abandoned the traditional procedure of language study. We now can no longer look for general notions such as energy, activity, labor, power of the spirit, world view, or expression, under which to submit language as a special case. Instead of explaining language in terms of one thing or another, and thus running away from it, the way to language intends to let language be experienced as language.* (OWL 119).

Heidegger follows the same approach that he takes to art. He selects examples and asks us to reflect on our experience of those examples. From within the experience of language, we will be better able to understand the nature of language. Heidegger's essays propose that language is best understood as saying. Moreover, saying always involves listening and belonging.

Speaking and Saying

Heidegger recognizes that when we think about language, we usually begin with the assumption that language is speaking. While he questions and challenges this assumption as it is normally understood, he also finds it an appropriate starting point for thinking about the nature of language. Sometimes Heidegger begins with our normal presuppositions in order to help us resist them. His review of our normal understandings of a thing serves this purpose. However, he begins with language as speaking, not only to show the problems with this presupposition but also because he thinks there is an insight hidden in this approach to language. Heidegger selects "A Winter Evening," a poem by Georg Trakl, as the example in his essay, "Language." He uses the example to explore what he calls the speaking of language.

In *Being and Time*, Heidegger interrogates Dasein in order to ask about Being. In inquiring into language he uses a similar approach, this time interrogating the poem. While Heidegger takes the poem as his guide, what concerns him is language. Because of this, any tolerably good poem might serve his purpose and providing the full poem is not necessary to understand how Heidegger uses the poem. The first two stanzas read:

> *Window with falling snow is arrayed.*
> *Long tolls the vesper bell,*
> *The house is provided well,*
> *The table is for many laid.*

> *Wandering ones, more than a few,*
> *Come to the door on darksome courses,*
> *Golden blooms the tree of graces*
> *Drawing us the earth's cool dew.* (PLT 194-95)

Heidegger says that the poem names the winter evening. It does this by calling the winter evening into words. The winter evening is not immediately present. In fact, the poem may be read on a hot summer day, and yet the presence of the winter evening is no less for its absence. Language speaks by naming, by calling things into a unique form of being present.

Moreover, Heidegger notes that what enters into words, in this case the winter evening, is not fully controlled by the words. If the words bring the thing into our presence, the thing still bears on us. It brings a

69

world with it. Reflecting on the poem shows us that what happens in speaking is that we say something. When we say something, we let it appear. We let something be seen and heard. However, Heidegger maintains that, "Even when Showing is accomplished by our human saying, even then this showing, this pointer, is preceded by an indication that it will let itself be shown" (OWL 123). Language is speaking and it does require human speaking, but if we are to say something, that is, to show, we must first listen. If language is saying which shows things and world, it requires listening and hearing.

Listening

Listening takes place in language. We are not able to hear something prior to its being said. So when we listen, we are letting something be said to us so that we can say it. Learning a second language illustrates this sort of listening. We listen intently so that we can hear how to say something. We want to say it correctly. Even inattentive listening illustrates Heidegger's point. We say things inaccurately when we have not listened well.

Certainly, Heidegger recognizes that much of our everyday speaking ignores the importance of listening. Yet, our way of speaking about such everyday talk indicates that we do understand the centrality of listening for saying something. We remark on many committee meetings that everyone talks, but no one has anything to say. We say that the teacher who drifts off topic and spends time discussing his or her personal life or interests during class has nothing to say.

In his essays on language, Heidegger usually focuses on listening in what he takes to be its most authentic forms. He maintains that listening is not passive receptivity. Listening is a type of activity that he characterizes as anticipation in reserve. He characterizes this activity in two seemingly polar ways. Listening is a keeping silent that is a pondering. It is also a speaking which is like singing.

The first type of listening is most appropriate for philosophy. The philosopher must hold back conceptual presuppositions in order to ponder words that present themselves in a text. The task of the philosopher is to listen to the text. The philosopher anticipates what is said not by presupposing a conceptual framework, but by questioning in such a way as to let the text speak. Indeed, Heidegger says that this listening tries to hear what is previously unsaid in the text. Listening attempts to hold open a space for the arrival of what has been hidden or concealed.

The second type of listening is most appropriate for poets. This listening is a sort of singing. If the philosopher must be careful to hold back concepts, the poet must send words out. The poet's form of listening is gathering and collecting words, setting them together, and offering them as a way for something to be shown, to show itself.

For Heidegger, both forms of listening show us that we belong in the world as speakers. He sometimes says that we reside or dwell in language.

Belonging

Heidegger connects residing or dwelling in language to *Ereignis*. In "The Way to Language" he writes, "Appropriation [*Ereignis*] grants to mortals their abode within their nature, so that they may be capable of being those who speak" (OWL 128). One of Heidegger's best explanations of *Ereignis* follows this quotation, clarifying what it means for humans to reside within their nature.

Heidegger says that *Ereignis* is a gentle law. It is a gathering that legislates and so enables all beings to be present in the manner in which they are most apt. Heidegger does not want to use language of a divine creation. That would certainly bring with it all kinds of metaphysical presuppositions that he wants to resist. Yet, the experience of language shows us that we are part of a totality. Moreover, there does seem to be a unique role for humans within that totality. To take up that role is to reside within the fullness of our nature. Our role is speaking. However, speaking is capable of being more than idle chatter. It can be saying.

In several of his later essays, Heidegger also develops the concept of dwelling to try to show what it means for humans to reside within the fullness of their nature. In "Building Dwelling Thinking," originally presented at a builder's convention, he says that the fundamental character of dwelling is sparing and preserving. He writes,

> *The sparing itself consists not only in the fact that we do not harm the one whom we spare. Real sparing is something <u>positive</u> and takes place when we leave something beforehand in its own nature, when we return it specifically to its being, when we "free" it in the real sense of the word into a preserve of peace. To dwell,*

71

to be set at peace, means to remain at peace within the free, the preserve, the free sphere that safeguards each thing in its nature. (PLT 149).

Heidegger maintains that we reside within our nature when we dwell poetically.

Poetry

The poetry of Hölderlin was especially important for Heidegger, and it is in one of Hölderlin's poems that Heidegger find the image of humans dwelling poetically. Heidegger maintains that this does not mean that the poetic is "merely an ornament and bonus added to dwelling" (PLT 215). Rather, poetry is what enables humans to really dwell. Poetry is what enables us to spare and preserve and safeguard things in their nature. It also enables us to measure ourselves.

Hans-Georg Gadamer believes that the question that guided all of Heidegger's thought is how to speak of God, especially after the thought of Nietzsche and the spiritual crisis of the early twentieth century. This insight is helpful for understanding the role that Heidegger gives to poetry and the poet.

While humans live in the everyday world, laboring and earning a living, what is fundamental to being human is something spiritual. If we are to dwell, to really be human, then we must take measure of ourselves in relation to this spiritual possibility. In order to do this, we must have some understanding of the holy, of what Heidegger comes to call the unknown god. Poetic images are able to reach out towards this holy and to hold open the possibility of this divine touching the human. Heidegger says,

> *This is why poetic images are imaginings in a distinctive sense: not mere fancies and illusions but imaginings that are visible inclusions of the alien in the sight of the familiar. The poetic saying of images gathers the brightness and sound of the heavenly appearances into one with the darkness and silence of what is alien. By such sights the god surprises us.* (PLT 226)

Poetry cannot cause the unknown god to come near, but poetry can put forward words that may enable this presence to show itself. It may be the case that this spiritual presence is only rarely experienced, but poetic dwelling calls us to be constantly heedful of the possibility.

In addition, Heidegger follows Hölderlin in suggesting that to dwell poetically is to keep kindness <u>with</u> our hearts (PLT 229). Heidegger emphasizes the importance of the word 'with.' In the absence of the holy, kindness serves as a measure for what it is to be human. We do not keep kindness <u>in</u> our hearts. Rather, kindness serves as the measure for how we dwell. To live so that kindness can show itself is to dwell poetically. We do not have to be poets to dwell poetically. However, Heidegger does indicate that we need poets if we are to learn how to dwell poetically. Poetry is a saying that is of fundamental importance for understanding what it is to be human and for living in the fullness of that understanding.

8

Science and Technology

Heidegger's concern for how we are to dwell also leads his thinking to issues of science and technology. In 1949 and 1950, he delivered four lectures that addressed the role of science and technology in shaping contemporary human life. The lectures were initially titled, "The Thing," "Enframing," "The Danger," and "The Turning." These were repeated and revised a number of times. The second lecture was eventually retitled, "The Question Concerning Technology." Heidegger continued to reflect on these issues throughout the 1950s. In 1962 he published a more extended account of the origin of contemporary science and its impact on our thinking, *What Is a Thing?* All of these works are helpful for understanding Heidegger's reflections on science and technology.

Heidegger approaches technology as a way of revealing the totality of beings. Technology frames the way in which we understand everything. Some people read Heidegger as rejecting technology and advocating a nostalgic return to a past free of technological inventions. He does think that the world is too full of airplanes and radios. He loves the country and the simplicity of agrarian life. However, Heidegger does not advocate opting out of technological aspects of life. Indeed, he does not even believe that this is possible.

Heidegger does not view technology as a foe of humans. It enables us to understand the world in which we live. In asking questions of technology, he suggests that technology poses a danger for human existence, but it also presents us with a saving power. It can serve to enable us to experience the fundamental role of humans in safeguarding beings in the world. Just as his thinking on language leads Heidegger to stress the importance of kindness, his reflections on technology lead him to stress the importance of safeguarding. Clearly, Heidegger's later work reaffirms the care structure of Dasein. In addition, his reflections on language and technology serve to clarify and develop his reflections on humanism.

Science and Mathematics

Philosophers and other humanists who reflect on science, mathematics, and technology are often accused of entering into areas for which they do not have the necessary expertise. They are described as romantic or charged with being ignorant and with lacking methodological rigor. In approaching Heidegger's reflections on science and mathematics, it is helpful to remember that he studied mathematics and natural science at the university level. He is knowledgeable of the content and method of contemporary science. His thought is based in that knowledge.

Heidegger acknowledges that modern science usually characterizes itself as factual, experimental, and as a form of investigation that calculates and measures. However, Heidegger maintains that this characterization overlooks the fundamental feature of science. Heidegger writes, "modern science is *mathematical*" (BW 249). While Heidegger recognizes that mathematics is usually understood as having to do with numbers, he suggests that we need to return to the fundamental meaning of mathematics to fully understand the role of science for contemporary thought.

In order to reflect on the mathematical as the fundamental feature of science, Heidegger calls on Greek thought. He explores both the derivation of the word 'mathematical' and Plato's emphasis on mathematics. He says that *ta mathēmata* means "what can be learned and thus, at the same time, what can be taught" (BW 250). In addition, he says that what can be learned is what we already know in some way. Because contemporary thinkers are accustomed to thinking about the mathematical in terms of numbers, this may seem a forced derivation. However, this is an example of the correctness of Heidegger's linguistic work. Any good dictionary confirms that the Greek word is primarily concerned with what can be learned.

Heidegger's interpretation does clearly reflect his thought in *Being and Time.* In order to understand something, we must already have some vague grasp of it. Heidegger says that "The mathematical is this fundamental position we take toward things by which we take up things as already given to us, and as they must and should be given" (BW 254). He maintains that Plato understood the mathematical in this way when he placed a sign over the entrance to his school, the Academy. The sign read, "Let no one who has not grasped the mathematical enter here!" In order to do academic work, in order to think, we must understand the presuppositions of our knowledge. We must have a grasp of the framework from within which we are able to learn and teach.

For modern thinkers, the framework that is presupposed in all learning is a scientific framework. This framework positions Dasein in two ways. It both frees and determines human thought.

Modern science frees human thought in that it moves our thinking out of the medieval framework dominated by revelation. Medieval thought, at least in the Western tradition, receives its presuppositions from Christian faith. The framework in which everything is thought is provided by revelation. This framework presupposes a dualism of transcendent reality and worldly existence. Worldly existence is always measured in terms of the transcendent, the other-worldly. Science, as it emerges with Galileo and Descartes, frees human thought from the control of the other-worldly by breaking with revelation. Modern science makes human reason and the human subject the foundation of all knowledge.

However, modern science does not simply free Dasein of medieval presuppositions. Science also changes, and in a sense determines, Dasein. It provides us with the presuppositions that frame all of our understanding. In medieval thought, humans were able to learn primarily through the opening of thought made possible by revelation. Whether or not there is a transcendent source of revelation, human learning in the medieval framework was based on the presupposition of such a source. While science frees us from this presupposition, it brings its own presupposition with which to frame human learning.

Modern science, as represented by the thought of Descartes, grounds knowledge in the human subject, the 'I.' This means that the subject is the fundamental presupposition against which everything else is learned, or measured. While modern science emphasizes that it is objective, it can only be objective because of the fundamental position of the subject. The subject is reason, "the court of appeal for the determination of the Being of beings, the thingness of things" (BW 282). Modern science makes possible modern technology, not because

76

technology is applied science, but because technology also depends on the fundamental position of the subject. In relation to this subject, things are disclosed as calculable and controllable. The framework for contemporary understanding of all that is is a technological framework.

Technology

The emergence of the age of technology involves this basic shift in what makes things accessible and intelligible to human understanding. The shift places the human at the center of reality. Everything is understood in relation to the fundamental position of the human. This is confirmed in everyday understandings of technology. We define technology in instrumental and anthropological ways. Technology is a means to an end that serves human desire. The computer is technological because it facilitates the exchange of information. In addition, we say that humans are technological when they can control technology. The person who can make the computer function is the technician and is said to have technological knowledge.

While this understanding seems obvious, Heidegger asks that we look more closely at technology. As he does with so many other issues, he asks questions in order to examine the experience of technology more fully. These questions lead him to the claim that, "Technology is a mode of revealing" (BW 295).

Technology as Enframing (Gestell)

Heidegger calls the mode of revealing that is characteristic of technology, enframing. The German word, *Gestell*, is the name for a skeleton and for a stand or a rack. Heidegger admits that this term seems strange. But he suggests that it functions similarly to Plato's use of the term 'idea.' Plato took a word from common speech that referred to the outward aspect of something and used it to articulate the essence of anything that is accessible. If for Plato it is the idea that makes possible all understanding, for modern humans it is technology as enframing that serves this function.

Technology, as this enframing, allows the world to be understood as raw material to be unlocked, exposed, and stored for human use. Technology demands that the things of the world give up their energy

77

and allow it to be stored or stockpiled. Things are ascribed value in terms of the energy that they can provide for human consumption.

Heidegger provides several examples that illustrate the shift in view that takes place when technology becomes the fundamental framework from which we learn and understand everything else. He notes that the peasant puts the fields in order, but this means caring and maintaining the fields. The peasant woman who wore the shoes that Van Gogh painted, cared for the land. Those who are engaged in agriculture within the context of technology challenge the land. Heidegger says, this agriculturist sets in order by setting-upon nature. Contemporary agriculture that produces genetic alterations of crops illustrates this approach even more fully. The genetic structure of the plants are exposed in order to produce "maximum yield at minimum expense" (BW 297).

Rivers, such as the Rhine, are understood as supplies of water and power. We build dams to release the power of the water. We arrange and transform rivers so that they can be a source of power for moving other natural resources. Even when we supposedly enjoy the natural beauty of the river, it is often as part of the travel industry. Heidegger describes the way in which technology sets the framework for our understanding of everything when he writes,

> The revealing that rules throughout modern technology has the character of a setting-upon, in the sense of a challenging-forth. Such challenging happens in that the energy concealed in nature is unlocked, what is unlocked is transformed, what is transformed is stored up, what is stored up is, in turn, distributed, and what is distributed is switched about ever anew. (BW 197-98)

Our total way of understanding occurs within the context of enframing, the standpoint of technology. We cannot escape or stand outside of this framework. If the framework challenges nature, it also challenges humans.

Technology and Destiny (Geschick)

Heidegger's thought suggests that technology is our destiny. The world into which we are born, or thrown, is a world that is structured in terms of the technological. As we live within this world, we are challenged to disclose the world in this context. A person born into the medieval world was challenged to understand the world as a divine creation. Those of us who are born into the contemporary world are challenged to understand in terms of this technological ordering. This way of understanding is a destining. Heidegger writes,

> *The essence of modern technology lies in enframing. Enframing belongs within the destining of revealing. These sentences express something different from the talk that we hear more frequently, to the effect that technology is the fate of our age, where "fate" means the inevitableness of an unalterable course.* (BW 307)

Technology is not our fate. This means that we do not have to blindly accept the framework of technology. However, it also means that our experience of technology may provide us with an option other than rebelling helplessly and cursing technology "as the work of the devil." We must respond to technology from within the context of the experience of technology. This is our contemporary destiny.

Responding to Technology

Heidegger sees two possible directions that we may take in responding to technology. These directions are not simply accepting or rejecting technology. If his analysis of our situation is correct, it is not possible for us to reject, or move outside of, the framework of technology. However, Heidegger does believe that our experience of technology can both show us the dangers of the technological framework and can show us the saving power that is still possible within that framework.

The Danger of Technology

Heidegger certainly recognizes that technology poses threats for human existence because it has enabled us to create such destructive weapons. Once we have extracted the energy from things and have this energy stockpiled, we are able to use it to destroy. We can commit mass slaughter of people and totally destroy the land and the vegetation that supports our existence. World War I exemplifies this possibility.

As the European countries developed weapons, they were moved in the direction of using them against each other. It was not that a few leaders were power hungry. The whole framework of understanding moved history towards the use of this tremendously destructive power. When we experience and recognize this very concrete danger that technology poses for us, we often respond by trying to master or control technology. However, this response only serves to confirm our drive to power. It does not enable us to change our framework of understanding.

While technology's capability to annihilate life is very real, Heidegger suggests that the greatest danger of technology is that it can so completely conceal our spiritual nature, our essence, that this will be lost to us. Two different tendencies within modern life both exhibit this danger that is inherent in the technological framework. While Heidegger does not specifically label these dangers, his descriptions make it clear that both capitalism and communism are products of the technological framework. Neither provides us with a pathway to experiencing our humanity.

Technology can lead us to believe that we are the lords of the earth. Examples of this position are abundant. We understand the things of the world and the world itself as functioning to meet our needs. We treat animals as sources of food and keep them confined in close and cruel compartments because the meat that is produced will taste better. We behave in ways that destroy life and even species, but firmly believe that this is our role. When we believe that we are lords, we lose sight of the truth that we are caught up in the claim of technology. We think we are lords when in truth we are situated finite beings, set on a direction by the framework that we are given.

Additionally, the framework of technology can lead us to take ourselves as raw material, as things to be stockpiled. We understand ourselves as sources of energy, of power. We understand ourselves as labor. We extract that energy and store it in the things that we make or in the capital that we create. We not only understand the things of the world in terms of the technological, we understand ourselves in that framework.

Both of these are dangers of technology because they threaten the very essence of what it is to be human. Yet, Heidegger does not believe that we should despair. He quotes Hölderlin,

But where danger is, grows
The saving power also. (BW 310)

80

The Saving Power of Technology

Heidegger maintains that if we experience technology in such a way that we recognize the dangers of technology, we are also positioned to recognize that technology is a mode of revealing. It is a framework that makes things accessible to us. Moreover, it is the framework that dominates our current capabilities to understand, and in Heidegger's terminology, to apprehend Being.

We also recognize that we are part of a totality such that we cannot easily and arbitrarily change this framework. We recognize that in the course of human history, the way in which Being has been understood has changed. The medieval framework is different from the modern technological framework. The change in frameworks is experienced as something given, not something manufactured or achieved. This understanding is the saving power. While clearly, technology could consume us, there is hope that it will not do so. Heidegger writes,

> *We look into the danger and see the growth of the saving power. Through this we are not yet saved. But we are thereupon summoned to hope in the growing light of the saving power. How can this happen? Here and now and in little things, that we may foster the saving power in its increase. This includes holding always before our eyes the extreme danger.* (BW 315)

What we can do is be open to the possibility of a different, and perhaps more appropriate, way of revealing.

Some people find in Heidegger's work an ecological direction. We need to live more simply and let beings, nature, reveal itself to us in ways that technology prevents. We must hold back from dominating things. Certainly, Heidegger's thought supports such thinking so long as it does not retain its basis in the supremacy of the human subject. Heidegger's main concern is that we move towards a more appropriate encounter with ourselves.

His own preference for how this can happen is in art. He thinks that art has historically been able to show us ourselves. He also thinks that art is considered so different from technology in our modern world, that it may have the greatest chance of not being dominated by the technological. In addition, or perhaps in relationship, to art, he also suggests that questioning is important. We must learn how to question and we must keep important questions before us. He says "questioning is the piety of thought" (BW 317).

81

Heidegger's early questions take him along a pathway that keep him constantly aware of the importance of asking who we are. The question of technology, again raises this question and challenges us to keep ourselves open to the question and the directions that it takes our thought and our lives.

9
Thinking

Heidegger's thought in the 1960s develops the implications of his questions concerning technology. From the beginning of his philosophical writings, he recognized the importance of asking questions. *Being and Time* begins with the question of how to raise the question of the meaning of being. Heidegger's essays develop by raising difficult and unusual questions. He maintains that questions need to be raised, not in order to obtain answers, but in order to provide paths for thinking.

Heidegger's questions take him along paths that trace the history of philosophy. He examines the beginnings of philosophy in the Greek thinker, Plato. In these beginnings, Heidegger sees philosophy taking the form of metaphysics. Metaphysics thinks about the world, about humanity, and about God. Heidegger says that metaphysics thinks beings as a whole in respect to Being.

Plato's thought began with philosophy as metaphysics. However, it also included the development of the sciences and their separation from philosophy. As the sciences emerge out of philosophy, they take on independence. Clear recent examples of this are the emergence of psychology and sociology as independent disciplines. These social sciences have separated from philosophy only in the last century.

Heidegger maintains that this development shows us something about the end, or completion of philosophy. Metaphysics opened a path for human thought that leads to modern sciences. These sciences share a fundamental attitude. Heidegger writes, "No prophecy is necessary to recognize that the sciences now establishing themselves will soon be determined and steered by the new fundamental science which is called cybernetics" (BW 376). Contemporary humans have arrived at the technological framework discussed in Chapter 8.

When Heidegger suggests that science and technology are the end of philosophy, he does not mean that these destroy philosophy. His use of the word 'end' relates to his contention that questions open paths. They set us going along paths. The path ends when we arrive at a destination. Contemporary thought, dominated by the technological, is the end that is our destination. Heidegger writes,

> The end of philosophy proves to be the triumph of the manipulable arrangement of a scientific-technological world and of the social order proper to this world. The end of philosophy means the beginning of the world civilization based upon Western European thinking. (BW 377)

Yet, Heidegger's reflections on technology clearly show that this framework threatens to destroy our spiritual nature. The world that technological thinking makes possible is one in which there are lords and laborers. In the face of this destination, Heidegger asks one more question.

What Task is Reserved for Thinking?

Heidegger's question is based on the possibility that there is a way of thinking that is neither metaphysical nor technological. Moreover, this possibility was there at the beginning of the path, but was not a possibility that philosophy could experience. It has remained hidden along the way. Heidegger says, it has been "reserved for thinking in a concealed way in the history of philosophy from its beginning to its end" (BW 377-78). Heidegger's essay, "The End of Philosophy and the Task of Thinking" gives some hints about this task. In reflecting on Heidegger's hints, it is important to remember that questions are paths. His hints are intended to set us to thinking, rather than to provide us with answers. He suggests that this thinking must be preparatory. It can still gain insight from phenomenology. It must meditate on opening and on unconcealment. It must surrender its previous thinking.

Thinking is Preparatory

Heidegger describes the task that is reserved for thinking as preparatory. This thinking will not found a new philosophical school or be heralded as the beginning of a new paradigm for understanding. Perhaps Heidegger is offering his own most ardent followers a hint here. There is not to be a Heideggarian school of thought as there is an Hegelian or an analytic school.

The thinking that is needed for our time must be unassuming. It must focus on what can be learned in the philosophical thought of the past, especially the Greeks. It does this in order to prepare for, or hold open the possibility of transformation. This thinking cannot predict the future. It might be described as an uncertain hoping. Heidegger says prepatory thinking holds open "the possibility that the world civilization which is just now beginning might one day overcome the technological-scientific-industrial character" (BW 379). This thought prepares for other possibilities for human understanding without knowing what those possibilities are.

Phenomenology

While philosophy is not the mode that this future thinking will take, it can still provide directive for the contemporary task of thinking. Heidegger has not abandoned the philosophical thought that served as the impetus for his work. His own philosophical work is not derivative of Husserl's work; yet, it is motivated by phenomenology. Phenomenology raises the call, "to the things themselves." Both Hegel and Husserl focused on subjectivity, and so focused on the presentation of things. Heidegger maintains that contemporary thinking must ask of phenomenology what still remains unthought in this call.

Opening (Lichtung)

According to Heidegger, what remains unthought in phenomenology is what he terms opening. He uses the word *Offenheit*, but then suggests that *Lichtung* is amore appropriate word. Heidegger is playing with the double meaning of 'light.' The English word carries a very similar complexity of meaning. The opening that must be thought is a lighting in the sense that things are brought into a clearing. Heidegger uses the image of a forest clearing to hint at what he means. When we walk out of the darkness of the forest, into a clearing, we experience this opening. Heidegger remarks that he does not mean the experience of brightness, but rather the experience of free space. He notes that for there to be brightness, there must first be the free space, the opening. This meaning is closer to the English sense of lightening, as in lightening a load. The opening is a space in which things are less dense.

Heidegger believes that we must become aware of and think this opening as the clear region in which things become both present and absent. He writes,

> *Accordingly, we may suggest that the day will come when we will not shun the question whether the opening, the free open, may not be that within which alone pure space and ecstatic time and everything present and absent in them have the place which gathers and protects everything.* (BW 385)

Heidegger not only believes that phenomenology points thinking in a helpful direction for thinking this opening, he also believes that the beginnings of philosophy also reflect the experience of this opening. However, the experience remains unthought.

Unconcealment (alētheia)

Heidegger returns to the pre-Socratic philosophers for a glimpse of the experience that is still unthought. He believes that Parmenides recorded the experience when he wrote,

> *...but you should learn all:*
> *the untrembling heart of unconcealment, well-rounded,*
> *and also the opinions of mortals*
> *who lack the ability to trust what is unconcealed.* (BW 387)

Heidegger translates the Greek *alētheia* as unconcealment. He used *alētheia* in *Being and Time* where he understood it to mean truth. However, in his reflections on what needs thinking at the end of the twentieth century, he resists understanding *alētheia* as truth. Instead, he suggests that unconcealment needs to be thought as the opening. Unconcealment is "the element in which Being and thinking and their belonging together exist" (BW 388).

Heidegger hopes that by trying to think *alētheia* in a manner that is prior to its meaning as truth, we may be able to experience something close to the experience that Parmenides reports. This experience may help us understand something more fundamental to the human relationship to Being than philosophical theories of truth have been able to provide. It may help us think the integral relationship of concealment and unconcealment.

Heidegger's hint about the need to think the opening as unconcealment emphasizes his earlier insights such as the relation of earth and world. He wants us to try to find ways to think how it is that we are intertwined with all that is. We belong together with everything that is. He recognizes that such thinking is difficult.

Surrender

Heidegger's emphasis on the importance of questions leads him to continually ask questions. Often he anticipates what his listeners or readers will ask. In relation to this call to think openness and *alētheia* he asks if all this talk is mysticism, mythology, or "ruinous irrationalism" (BW 391). He knows that those thinkers who have been educated in the rigors of contemporary philosophy will find his approach questionable. Many philosophers accuse Heidegger of being incomprehensible and irrational. They suggest that his later thought is mystical and dominated by the religious.

Heidegger is aware of these accusations, but he persists in asking us to consider the sort of thinking that he proposes. He writes,

> *Perhaps there is a thinking which is more sober-minded than the incessant frenzy of rationalization and the intoxicating quality of cybernetics. One might aver that it is precisely this intoxication that is extremely irrational.* (BW 391)

Heidegger suggests that the most immediate task for us may be to surrender previous thinking and take the risk of the sort of thinking that he suggests. Heidegger read the Danish existentialist thinker, Søren Kierkegaard during his early education. Kierkegaard's influence is evident in *Being and Time*, especially in Heidegger's emphasis on freedom and death. Kierkegaard was a religious thinker who emphasized the importance of what he called a 'leap of faith' that is vital for full human existence. Heidegger returns to Kierkegaard's language of a leap to explain the sort of surrender that is needed for thinking. He writes,

> *...we are attempting to learn thinking. The way is long. We dare take only a few steps. If all goes well, they will take us to the foothills of thought. But they will take us to places which we must explore to reach the point where only the leap will help further. The leap alone takes us into the neighborhood where thinking resides.* (BW 353)

In the end, Heidegger's thought is not a school of philosophy but an attempt to point us in a direction in preparation for a leap to a more fully human way of thinking.

Thinking After Heidegger

At the burial of Martin Heidegger, Bernhard Welte, a Catholic priest and Professor of Christian Philosophy of Religion at the University of Freiburg, said of Heidegger,

> *He was always seeking and always underway. At various times he emphatically characterized his thinking as a path. He traveled this path without ceasing. There were bends and turns along it, certainly there were stretches where he went astray. Heidegger always understood the path as one that was given to him, sent to him. He sought to understand his word as a response to an indication to which he listened without respite. For him, to think was to thank, to make grateful response to that appeal.* (Sheehan 73)

The best way to evaluate Heidegger's work may be from the tasks and paths that it sets for thinking. In this respect, his thinking has been fruitful. It has influenced contemporary Christian theology, especially through the work of Rudolf Bultmann and John Macquarrie. It has given impetus to a direction in philosophy known as philosophical hermeneutics, particularly in the work of Hans-Georg Gadamer. It has influenced literary criticism and the movement in contemporary thought called deconstruction. Both Jacque Derrida and Luce Irigary, contemporary French thinkers, owe much to Heidegger's work. In addition, his thinking has stirred thought about human responsibility to the environment. And, it has made us think seriously about the relation of philosophy and politics.

If his thinking enables us to meditate on and so better understand what it is to be finite and yet spiritual, then, no matter what we think of some of the turns that he took, our paths will have been enriched through his thinking.

Glossary

Glossary

Auslegung	interpretation
Befindilichkeit	disposition, mood
Besorge	concern
Dasein	There being; the being that is in each case mine
Entschlossenheit	resoluteness
Ereignis	event
Erschlossenheit	disclosedness
Fürsorge	solicitude
Geschehen	happen, occur
Geschichtlichkeit	historicality
Geschick	destiny
Gestell	enframing
In-der-Welt-sein	Being-in-the –world
Kehre	turn
Lichtung	lighting, opening, clearing
Riss	rift
Seiendes	entities, beings
Sein	Being
Sorge	care
Sprache	language
Verstehen	understanding
Vorhandenes	present at hand
Zuhandenes	handy

Bibliography

Selected English Translations of Heidegger's Writing

Basic Problems of Phenomenology. Trans. Albert Hofstadter. Bloomington, IN: Indiana UP, 1982.

Basic Writings. Ed. David Farrell Krell. New York: Harper and Row, 1977. (Where possible citations are from this volume)

Being and Time. Trans. John Macquarrie & Edward Robinson. New York: Harper and Row, 1962. (All quotations from BT are from this translation.)

Being and Time. Trans. Joan Stambaugh. Albany, NY: SUNY Press, 1996.

The Concept of Time. Trans. William McNeill. Oxford: Blackwell, 1992.

Early Greek Thinking. Trans. David Farrell Krell and Frank A. Capuzzi. New York: Harper and Row, 1975.

The End of Philosophy. Trans. Joan Stambaugh. New York: Harper and Row, 1973.

The Essence of Reasons. Trans. Terrence Malick. Evanston, IL: Northwestern UP, 1969.

Kant and the Problem of Metaphysics. Trans. James S. Churchill. Bloomington, IN: Indiana UP, 1962.

Nietzsche, Vols I-III. Trans. David Farrell Krell. New York, Harper and Row, 1979, 1984, and 1987.

On the Way to Language. Trans. Peter D. Hertz. New York, Harper and Row, 1971.

On Time and Being. Trans. Joan Stambaugh. New York: Harper and Row, 1972.

Poetry, Language, Thought. Trans. Albert Hofstadter. New York: Harper and Row, 1971.

Pathmarks. Ed. William McNeill. New York: Cambridge UP, 1998.

The Question Concerning Technology and Other Essays. Trans. William Lovitt. New York: Harper and Row, 1977.

What is a Thing? Trans. W. B. Barton and Vera Deutsch. Chicago: Regnery, 1969.

What is Called Thinking? Trans. Fred D. Wieck and J. Glenn Gray. New

York: Harper and Row, 1968.

Abbreviaitions

BT   *Being and Time* (All page numbers refer to the German pages.)
BW   *Basic Writings*
EGT   *Early Greek Thinking*
OWL *On the Way to Language*
PLT   *Poetry, Language, Thought*

Selected Books and Anthologies

Bindeman, Steven L. *Heidegger and Wittgenstein: The Poetics of Silence.* Washington, DC: University Press of America, 1981.

Dreyfus, Hubert L. *Being-in-the-World A Commentary of Heidegger's "Being and Time," Division I.* Cambridge, MA: MIT Press, 1991.

Gadamer, Hans-Georg. *Heidegger's Ways.* Trans. John W. Stanley. Albany, NY: SUNY Press, 1994.

Guignon, Charles B, ed. *The Cambridge Companion to Heidegger.* New York: Cambridge UP, 1993.

Kisiel, Theodore. *The Genesis of Heidegger's Being and Time.* Berkeley: University of California P, 1993.

Kockelmans, Joseph J., ed. *On Heidegger and Language.* Evanston, IL: Northwestern UP, 1972.

Langan, Thomas. *The Meaning of Heidegger.* New Yorik: Columbia UP, 1961.

Macquarrie, John. *Heidegger and Christianity.* London: SCM Press, 1994.

Marx, Werner. *Heidegger and the Tradition.* Trans. Theodore Kisiel and Murray Greene. Evanston, IL: Northwestern UP, 1971.

Murray, Michael, ed. *Heidegger and Modern Philosophy.* New Haven, CN: Yale UP, 1978.

Neske, Günther and Emil Kettering. *Martin Heidegger and National Socialism, Questions and Answers.* Trans. Lisa Harries and Joachim Neugroschel. New York: Paragon House, 1990.

Ott, Hugo. *Martin Heidegger, A Political Life.* Trans. Allan Blunden. New York: Basic Books, 1993.

Richardson, William J., SJ. *Heidegger, Through Phenomenology to Thought.* The Hague: Martinus Nijhoff, 1974.

Rockmore, Tom. *The Heidegger Case, On Philosophy and Politics.* Philadelphia: Temple UP, 1992.

Sheehan, Thomas. *Heidegger, The Man and the Thinker.* Chicago: Precedent Publishing, 1981.

Pöggeler, Otto. *The Paths of Heidegger's Life and Thought.* Trans. John Bailiff. Amherst, NY: Humanity Books, 1998